KT-199-241

TOTAL TRIVIA

TOTAL TRIVIA

Martin Plimmer

with
**Roger Millington,
Joyce Robins and George Smith**

First published in 1985 by
Octopus Books Limited
59 Grosvenor Street, London W1

Second impression, 1986

© 1985 Hennerwood Publications Limited

ISBN 0 86273 262 X

Made and printed in Great Britain
by Richard Clay (The Chaucer Press) Ltd
Bungay, Suffolk

CONTENTS

FOREWORD

'What is the name of the river Thames?'

That was the first quiz question I can remember hearing and it's certainly the first one I got right. Admittedly my parents gave me a little help, but not that much.

I have always enjoyed quizzes ever since an inspired geography teacher lined our whole class up along a wall and proceeded to ask us one by one the capitals of the world. I went right from the bottom to the top of the class in one go as my superiors failed to answer 'Juneau the capital of Alaska?'. As you can see, I don't just like quizzes, I like puns too.

These two were, of course, silly, joky questions. But recently the very word trivia and/or trivial, with its self-mocking overtones, has in some way made general knowledge quizzes — just like crosswords — intellectually acceptable. Those of us who before have felt excluded from the crossword club have now come into our own. Us 'trivies' have, if anything, a slight disdain for the *truly* trivial, lateral thinking, masochistic verbalists — the crossworders.

I once saw my name in the answers section for the *Radio Times* crossword. Even then, armed with the answer, I was unable to understand the clue — 'Merrily took boat to pieces, for the entertainer'. A crossworder friend admitted the clue was perhaps a little unfair as the word 'entertainer' was so misleading! Some friend!

Of course it is the mixed categories in the trivia books and games which have made them so attractive. Everyone is now in with a chance and I think the compilers of our *Total Trivia* have got it absolutely right, with the fairest categories yet. And I particularly like question 10 in Trivia Quiz 6.

My own piece of advice is *never* say, 'I don't know'. *Always* have a guess. A friend of mine at Cambridge once answered, 'Aristotle' to six questions in a round of University Challenge – they were in fact the *only* six answers he gave – but two of them were right. A little intelligence is required because quite clearly 'Aristotle' will not be the answer to, 'How fast can penguins fly?' But what, for example, if the question were, 'Name Jackie Kennedy's second husband'?

Have fun with this book. I'm sure you will with questions as varied as, 'Which is older, Barbie or Sindy?' and, 'What is Margaret Thatcher's middle name?' (No rude answers please.) And what can possibly be the question to which the answer is, 'Yes – it means they share the same tent'?

And yes, crossworders can play too.

INTRODUCTION

What's the most common answer to any question? It is probably 'I don't know', though I wouldn't like to have to prove it.

You'll find when you play this book that a small proportion of the questions here will also provoke that answer. The odd problem that would have made Einstein pause for a moment's reflection, adds spice to a quiz.

I wouldn't be giving too much away, for instance, if I told you that one question in this book is almost impossible, unless you happen to live in Llanfairpwllgwyngyllgogerychwyrndrobwllllanty-siliogogogoch, in which case you would have an unfair advantage. By the way, the name of that Welsh town is part of the answer to that particular question, but it's no use trying to memorise the spelling, because unless you're the Brain of Britain, or psychic, you won't be able to identify the question to which it is the answer.

That's not to say all the questions here are stinkers. Far from it. At the other extreme there are a few that are simply...well, simple, like: what colour are London buses? and: how many pennies were there in an old pound? They are so easy they would make Einstein turn in his grave. They are also the sort of questions that land plum in your lap just when you need them most in this game, giving you a valuable lead on points and making your competitors writhe on the carpet in envy.

Life without this second sort of question, unless you are the Brain of Britain, or psychic, or a resident of Llanfairpwllgwyngyll-gogerychwyrndrobwllllantysiliogogogoch, would just be intolerable for most of us.

Between these two extremes you'll find the great bulk of questions; the ones that frustrate and entice quiz addicts in equal measure, making a book like this as hard to put down as a high voltage cable.

They are the sort of question to which you definitely know the answer (in fact you were talking about it just the other day) but for some obtuse reason you can't locate exactly where you filed it in the GCHQ of your mind.

Most of us carry more trivial information in our heads than exists in a million volumes like this one. We might know, for instance, that it's illegal to be left-handed in Albania, that the Ethiopian

Emperor Menelik II restored his health by eating pages of the Bible, or that the Basques speak a tongue unconnected to any other European language, but we file all this information away in much the same way it comes to us — haphazardly.

You may *know* that an answer to a question about the equatorial rain forest is in your head somewhere — you can remember hearing it on that visit to Disneyland—but in order to track it down in the memory vaults you might have to follow a cross-reference to a file marked 'Lunar Space Probe' and a sub-section labelled 'Donald Duck'.

It is this mental detective work that makes the hunt for renegade answers to irrelevant questions so tantalizing. Satisfaction arrives with the unearthing of a long forgotten item of information exactly fitting a question, from some particularly dusty corner. And, of course, it's the effort of trying to do all this better than your white-knuckled competitors that makes it so exciting.

There is another kind of question that falls between the Albert Einstein and Stan Laurel levels. It is ostensibly a harder or more specialized question, but it is phrased in such a way that it is actually loaded with clues. Wit and cunning are as important as memory in these matters. You may not *know* this answer, but a little rattling of the grey matter might well dislodge it.

For instance, being suddenly faced with a word like 'triskaide-kaphobia' may leave you gasping in temporary panic, but with steady nerves, an elementary knowledge of languages and some calculated guesswork, you can pull the word apart and deduce that it means 'fear of the number 13'. (Don't bank on triskaidekaphobia cropping up, by the way, because that's the last you'll hear of it in this book.)

You will notice that there are 13 questions in each quiz, two of which are miscellaneous and one of which is a quizmaster question: not necessarily a harder question, but one which we think is so intriguing that it merits a starring role, so special in fact, that we think a correct answer to a quizmaster question should be rewarded by bonus points. The other categories are based on:

GEOGRAPHY AND TRAVEL, which is really self-explanatory;

PEOPLE, those within living memory, including some pretty zany human achievements;

INVENTIONS, which also covers discoveries and technology;

HISTORY, which is another category that defines itself;

SPORT, this includes some leisure, food and hobby interests which definitely wouldn't qualify as sports at the Olympics;

MUSIC, which covers all sorts, from pop to country to classical;

SCIENCE, the one I'd always want to avoid;

THE ARTS, largely literature, but with a generous sprinkling of visual arts questions as well;

FILM, TV AND RADIO, the test of how much we *really* watch and listen;

NATURAL HISTORY, another one at which I'm a dunce.

Of course this book can be enjoyed in private by all closet quiz addicts, but we have devised several games which we believe will provide even more fun for two or more players. However, if you all want to be friends at the end of a game, you should interpret each other's answers generously.

I can't honestly say that playing this book is educational, because most of the new information it will cram into your already overcrowded head will be of no earthly use to you ever again. But I will make one claim, and this claim is also a criterion against which each question chosen for this book has been judged.

I know that in the end, your enjoyment will derive less from the answers you know, than from those you don't know. Why? Well, the answer to that one is easy: because they are fascinating questions and I can guarantee that the answers will delight you.

MARTIN PLIMMER

QUIZ GAME 1

Two opposing players, pairs or teams.

1. Before the game begins, each player selects their own special subject (not miscellany and quizmaster). When a player answers questions on that particular subject correctly, he or she earns a higher score (see below). Both players can select the same special subject. One person should keep the score.

2. Players take it in turn to ask each other a single quiz (i.e. a set of 13 questions) and the scores are noted down. Depending on time available, the game can last as long as you want, though it's more exciting if you decide how many turns constitute a game before you start. The person with the highest score when this point is reached is the winner.

3. Each correct answer is scored as follows: miscellany = 1; individual player's special subject = 5; all other subjects except quizmaster = 2; quizmaster = double the player's score for that turn (i.e. double his or her score for 12 questions).

4. If a player scores 50 in a single turn (i.e. gets all 13 questions right), he or she wins the game outright.

5. A strict time limit of 30 seconds per question should be set, or less if you want the game to go faster. Answers should be interpreted generously.

QUIZ GAME 2

The same as Game 1, but with these variations:

1. Players cannot have the same special subject. Before the game begins, each player cuts a pack of cards. The person with the highest card has first choice of special subject (apart from miscellany and quizmaster). The person with the second highest card has second choice etc. In the event of a draw, players cut again. The card ranking runs king (highest), queen, knave, ten, down to ace (lowest).

2. At any stage in the game two players can swap or barter subjects in their possession provided they both consent.

3. Ignore rule 4 in Game 1. If a player scores 35 or more in a single turn (a set of 13 questions), he or she can select another special subject from the subjects still left, to add to the one already held, and from then on that subject too, will score him or her five points for every correct answer. Players can continue amassing special subjects like this (provided they score 35 or more in a single turn) until all the subjects are used up. Only when subjects 2 to 11 are all allocated, can the two miscellany categories be used as special subjects. The first player to take a miscellany as a special subject must specify either miscellany 1 or miscellany 12. Correctly answered special subject miscellany questions also score five points.

QUIZ GAME 3

For two or more players or teams.

1. One person should keep the scores.

2. The game is played category by category. The first player asks the next player on the left a question from the first miscellany section of Quiz 1. That player in turn asks the next player on the left a miscellany question from Quiz 2 and so on until all the players have been asked a miscellany question. The next round is geography, the next people and so on through the 13 sections.

3. Players are allowed to select a specialist subject before starting as in Game 1, rule 1. Score as in Game 1, rule 3.

4. Each player can double his or her entire score for the game by a correct quizmaster answer.

5. If a player gets a question wrong or fails to answer it, it must be offered to the next player, who on answering correctly gains the points the previous player would have had (1, 2 or 5 – see Game 1, rule 3). The player then proceeds to answer his or her own question.

TRIVIA QUIZ 1

1 MISCELLANY: What business did brothers Maurice and Charles start in 1970 to become the world's fifth largest of its type by 1985?

2 GEOGRAPHY & TRAVEL: By what name was Kampuchea formerly known?

3 PEOPLE: What is Margaret Thatcher's middle name?

4 INVENTIONS: What piece of bent wire, invented by Johann Vaaler in 1899, replaced the pin and the ribbon?

5 HISTORY: What did Pope Pius V do to Queen Elizabeth in 1570?

6 SPORT: How many games in a rubber of contract bridge?

7 MUSIC: Which group named itself after an American firetruck?

8 SCIENCE: Which has more calories, fat or sugar?

9 THE ARTS: What did Phileas Fogg do and how long did it take him?

10 FILM, TV & RADIO: Which rock star could only be shown on America's *Ed Sullivan Show* from the waist up?

11 NATURAL HISTORY: How long, to the nearest 50 years, has the dodo been dead?

12 MISCELLANY: Who was forced into a hairdressing job by his mother, although it was the last thing he wanted to do?

▶ **QUIZMASTER:** Who was Big Ben named after?

TRIVIA QUIZ 2

1 MISCELLANY: How many old pennies in a pound?

2 GEOGRAPHY & TRAVEL: On which city estate are Europe's highest residential towers?

3 PEOPLE: What is the highest Soviet decoration?

4 INVENTIONS: What material were World War II troop-carrying gliders made of?

5 HISTORY: What was the longest war in history?

6 SPORT: Where is the Bernebeu Stadium?

7 MUSIC: Which composer and pianist also became Prime Minister of Poland?

8 SCIENCE: How many sides does a heptagon have?

9 THE ARTS: Who lived at Tara?

10 FILM, TV & RADIO: Which famous radio comic called his programme his '*Halfhour*'?

11 NATURAL HISTORY: The aardvark was named by Dutch settlers in Africa. What does the name mean?

12 MISCELLANY: What was Lord Louis Mountbatten's relationship to Queen Victoria?

▶ **QUIZMASTER:** What do the following have in common: Sussex Pond, Cabinet and Eve's?

ANSWERS 1

1 Saatchi & Saatchi.

2 Cambodia.

3 Hilda.

4 The paper clip.

5 He excommunicated her.

6 Three.

7 REO Speedwagon.

8 Fat.

9 He went round the world in 80 days.

10 Elvis Presley.

11 304 years.

12 Vidal Sassoon.

■ Sir Benjamin Hall, Commissioner Of Works at the time the Houses Of Parliament were built.

ANSWERS 2

1 240.

2 The Barbican, London.

3 The Order of Lenin.

4 Plywood.

5 The Hundred Years War (which actually lasted for 115 years).

6 Barcelona.

7 Paderewski.

8 Seven.

9 The O'Haras in *Gone With The Wind*.

10 Tony Hancock.

11 Earth-pig.

12 He was her great-grandson.

■ They are all names of British puddings.

TRIVIA QUIZ 3

1 MISCELLANY: Which American president won the biggest vote in American election history?

2 GEOGRAPHY & TRAVEL: What is the main manufacturing industry of Detroit?

3 PEOPLE: Who was cast adrift from *The Bounty* after a mutiny?

4 INVENTIONS: How many lines has a British TV transmission?

5 HISTORY: What did British motorists have to contend with for the first time in 1960?

6 SPORT: What is pontoon called when it's played in a casino?

7 MUSIC: Who was Eric Clapton yearning for in his love song 'Layla'?

8 SCIENCE: What in astronomy is indicated by the mnemonic 'Men Very Easily Make Jugs Serving Useful Necessary Purposes?'

9 THE ARTS: John Harmon is the hero of which Dickens' novel?

10 FILM, TV & RADIO: Which TV series ends every episode with bedroom lights being switched off and a family wishing each other goodnight?

11 NATURAL HISTORY: What is the largest carnivore on land?

12 MISCELLANY: How many years are there in a sesquicentenary?

► QUIZMASTER: What is the longest word you can type, using only the letters on the top line of a typewriter (QWERTYUIOP)?

TRIVIA QUIZ 4

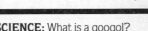

1 MISCELLANY: What culinary treat did John Montagu, a compulsive 18th century gambler invent, so that he didn't have to leave the gaming tables?

2 GEOGRAPHY & TRAVEL: On the shore of which lake are Chicago and Milwaukee?

3 PEOPLE: Who was the last woman hanged in England?

4 INVENTIONS: Who is reputed to have invented the googly?

5 HISTORY: Why are policemen called bobbies?

6 SPORT: Which cricketer won his England cap before his county cap?

7 MUSIC: Who or what sang to Beatrice Harrison's cello accompaniment in a famous early BBC outside broadcast?

8 SCIENCE: What is a googol?

9 THE ARTS: Whose biography did James Boswell write in 1791?

10 FILM, TV & RADIO: Which TV talent show used a 'clapometer' to select winners?

11 NATURAL HISTORY: What sea fossils can be found in the Himalayas at the height of 18,000 feet?

12 MISCELLANY: Which eminent Labour politician is a devoted supporter of Sheffield Wednesday?

► QUIZMASTER: On what condition did Jeremy Bentham will his money to the University College Hospital, London?

ANSWERS 3

1 Ronald Reagan.

2 Motor cars.

3 Captain Bligh.

4 625.

5 Traffic wardens.

6 Blackjack.

7 Former model Patti Boyd, at that time wife of George Harrison.

8 The initials of planets, going outwards from the Sun (Mercury, Venus, Earth, Mars, Jupiter, Saturn, Uranus, Neptune, Pluto).

9 *Our Mutual Friend.*

10 *The Waltons.*

11 The polar bear.

12 150.

■ Proprietory.

ANSWERS 4

1 The Sandwich (he was the Fourth Earl of Sandwich).

2 Lake Michigan.

3 Ruth Ellis.

4 B.J.T. Bosanquet, Reginald Bosanquet's father.

5 They are named after the founder of the Metropolitan Police, Sir Robert Peel.

6 Brian Close in 1949.

7 Nightingales.

8 A very large number; one followed by 100 zeros.

9 Dr Johnson's.

10 Hughie Green's *Opportunity Knocks.*

11 Ammonites.

12 Roy Hattersley.

■ That his body be preserved and brought in to all board meetings.

TRIVIA QUIZ 5

1 MISCELLANY: What does onomatopoeia mean?

2 GEOGRAPHY & TRAVEL: Lake Superior straddles the border of which two countries?

3 PEOPLE: What was Charles Blondin's claim to fame?

4 INVENTIONS: Why do you not see the whole picture when watching films on TV?

5 HISTORY: What did the 1944 Education Act extend to all?

6 SPORT: In cricket, how far is the popping crease from the stumps?

7 MUSIC: Which American star once worked as a race track groom, kennel maid and karate lesson salesgirl, when all she wanted to do was have fun?

8 SCIENCE: What infrequent astronomical phenomenon will take place above Britain on August 11, 1999?

9 THE ARTS: What was the name of the boat in which Gulliver was shipwrecked?

10 FILM, TV & RADIO: Auntie Vi from *Nursery Sing-Song* went on to become a favourite character in a TV soap opera. Who was she?

11 NATURAL HISTORY: What is the name of the two-humped camel?

12 MISCELLANY: What is the common name of *Squatina angelus*, a fish which has become popular in Britain since the 70s?

▶ **QUIZMASTER:** Which 19th century artist was awarded a farthing in a libel case?

TRIVIA QUIZ 6

1 MISCELLANY: A female toad will produce 20,000 of them in one session. What are they?

2 GEOGRAPHY & TRAVEL: Which lies further south, Marbella or Algiers?

3 PEOPLE: Which country has the world's highest divorce rate?

4 INVENTIONS: What do Clifton Suspension Bridge, Rotherhithe Tunnel and the *Great Eastern* have in common?

5 HISTORY: Which small, burrowing animal caused the death of William III?

6 SPORT: Name one of the numbers either side of three in darts.

7 MUSIC: Henry Rowley Bishop was most famous for composing which popular song?

8 SCIENCE: What does the sign ∴ mean to a mathematician?

9 THE ARTS: What was the name of Billy Bunter's school?

10 FILM, TV & RADIO: Which '60s radio show with John Cleese and Tim Brooke-Taylor featured ferrets, rhubarb tarts and wombats?

11 NATURAL HISTORY: What is the world's largest animal?

12 MISCELLANY: Which edible vegetable relative of the sunflower has nothing to do with the artichoke and doesn't come from The Middle East?

▶ **QUIZMASTER:** Who died in the arms of the last German Kaiser?

ANSWERS 5

1 It is the term used to describe a word whose sound mimics the thing or action it describes.

2 Canada and The United States of America.

3 He crossed Niagara Falls on a tightrope.

4 Because the TV screen is square, the 35mm (oblong) film print has to be cropped.

5 Secondary education.

6 Four feet.

7 Cyndi Lauper.

8 The next total eclipse.

9 *The Antelope*.

10 Violet Carson (who played Ena Sharples).

11 The bactrian camel.

12 Monkfish.

■ Whistler (against Ruskin).

ANSWERS 6

1 Eggs.

2 Marbella.

3 America.

4 They were all built by Isambard Kingdom Brunel.

5 A mole; his horse tripped on a molehill and threw him.

6 17 or 19.

7 'Home Sweet Home'.

8 Because.

9 Greyfriars.

10 *I'm Sorry I'll Read That Again*.

11 The blue whale (it can reach a length of 110 feet and weight of 170 tons).

12 The Jerusalem artichoke.

■ Queen Victoria.

TRIVIA QUIZ 7

1 MISCELLANY: How many sides does a 50p coin have?

2 GEOGRAPHY & TRAVEL: Which river runs through Cambridge?

3 PEOPLE: In America, what does a realtor do?

4 INVENTIONS: What building material was used extensively by the Romans and then forgotten until the 18th century?

5 HISTORY: Which organization was founded by William Booth?

6 SPORT: What board game is known as 'The Game Of The Four Winds'?

7 MUSIC: What did Mr Bojangles do to amuse his cell mates?

8 SCIENCE: Who established horse-power as a unit of measurement?

9 THE ARTS: What was the eventual title of a book which was originally called 'Incident At West Egg'?

10 FILM, TV & RADIO: *Man About The House* characters later appeared in two other spin-off situation comedies. What were they?

11 NATURAL HISTORY: How fast (to the nearest 10 mph) can a racing pigeon fly in still air?

12 MISCELLANY: Which London theatre and opera house is built on the site of a well once famous for its medicinal properties?

▶ QUIZMASTER: By what more familiar title is the First Lord Of The Treasury known?

TRIVIA QUIZ 8

1 MISCELLANY: In post-war fashion, who was responsible for the 'New Look'?

2 GEOGRAPHY & TRAVEL: What or where is Europa?

3 PEOPLE: Which Prime Minister said ' a week is a long time in politics'?

4 INVENTIONS: Which new leisure activity was handed to the world on a plate by an American pie company around 1900?

5 HISTORY: In what year did Concorde first fly?

6 SPORT: Which London stadium is a venue for both football and greyhound racing?

7 MUSIC: Who first said 'Awop-bop-a-loo-mop-alop-bam-boom'?

8 SCIENCE: Name two inert gasses.

9 THE ARTS: What was the name of Don Quixote's horse?

10 FILM, TV & RADIO: Which Welsh village provided the setting for *The Prisoner*?

11 NATURAL HISTORY: What animal became extinct in Britain in 1683?

12 MISCELLANY: Why did Australian judge 'Diamond Jim' McClelland come to London in 1984?

▶ QUIZMASTER: Which famous London street name contains six consonants unseparated by vowels?

ANSWERS 7

1 Seven.

2 The Cam.

3 He's an estate agent.

4 Concrete.

5 The Salvation Army.

6 Mah Jong.

7 He danced.

8 James Watt.

9 *The Great Gatsby.*

10 *Robin's Nest* and *George And Mildred.*

11 About 60 mph.

12 Sadler's Wells.

■ The Prime Minister.

ANSWERS 8

1 Christian Dior.

2 One of Jupiter's 14 moons.

3 Harold Wilson.

4 The frisbee. Customers who bought Frisbee Pies discovered that the tins made excellent projectiles.

5 1969.

6 Wembley.

7 Little Richard singing 'Tutti Frutti', in 1955.

8 Argon, helium, neon, krypton, xenon, radon.

9 Rosinante.

10 Portmeirion.

11 Wild boar.

12 To head the Royal Commission investigating the effects of British nuclear tests in Australia.

■ Knightsbridge.

TRIVIA QUIZ 9

1 MISCELLANY: Which fish can kill by electrocution?

2 GEOGRAPHY & TRAVEL: Which British theatre has a permanent backdrop of sea and sky?

3 PEOPLE: What is the name for someone who studies bird life?

4 INVENTIONS: Where was the word robot first used?

5 HISTORY: Where was Napoleon Bonaparte born?

6 SPORT: Who scored the dramatic fourth goal in the 1953 cup final between Blackpool and Bolton?

7 MUSIC: Which opera tells the story of a girl who works in a cigarette factory?

8 SCIENCE: What are the Perseids?

9 THE ARTS: Whose first play was *Widowers' Houses*?

10 FILM, TV & RADIO: Which 1966 drama/documentary led to the establishment of Shelter, the charity for the homeless?

11 NATURAL HISTORY: What was the Duke of Wellington's reply when Queen Victoria asked him how to rid the Crystal Palace of sparrows?

12 MISCELLANY: How fast can a penguin fly?

▶ **QUIZMASTER:** Which popular association was originally called 'the Rosebuds'?

TRIVIA QUIZ 10

1 MISCELLANY: Which postman has a cat called Jesse?

2 GEOGRAPHY & TRAVEL: Which two oceans are joined by the Bering Strait?

3 PEOPLE: Who provided the original voice for Mickey Mouse?

4 INVENTIONS: Which EEC member uses more microwave ovens than the rest put together?

5 HISTORY: Who led the British movement for votes for women?

6 SPORT: In Monopoly, what completes a set with Fleet Street and The Strand?

7 MUSIC: Which musical is based on the poems of T.S. Eliot?

8 SCIENCE: Which point did Scotsman John Napier introduce in a book in 1617?

9 THE ARTS: Who painted the ceiling of the Sistine Chapel?

10 FILM, TV & RADIO: Which soap opera is mostly set in Albert Square?

11 NATURAL HISTORY: What common rodent did the Normans bring over with them to Britain?

12 MISCELLANY: Which Indian smoked fish and rice recipe was adopted by the 19th century British as a breakfast dish?

▶ **QUIZMASTER:** Which Prime Minister felled trees for a hobby?

ANSWERS 9

1 The electric eel.

2 The Minack Theatre of Cornwall.

3 An ornithologist.

4 In Czech Karel Capek's 1923 play *R.U.R.* (Rossum's Universal Robots). Robota in Czechoslovakian means compulsory service.

5 Corsica.

6 Bill Perry

7 *Carmen.*

8 Summer meteor showers.

9 George Bernard Shaw's.

10 *Cathy Come Home.*

11 'Sparrowhawks, Ma'am'.

12 Penguins cannot fly.

■ The Brownies.

ANSWERS 10

1 Postman Pat.

2 The Pacific and the Arctic.

3 Walt Disney.

4 Great Britain.

5 Emmeline Pankhurst.

6 Trafalgar Square.

7 *Cats.*

8 The decimal point.

9 Michelangelo.

10 *Eastenders.*

11 The rabbit.

12 Kedgeree.

■ William Gladstone.

TRIVIA QUIZ 11

1 MISCELLANY: Which English humorist's Christian names were Pelham Grenville?

2 GEOGRAPHY & TRAVEL: Which country had Asia's fastest growing economy during the 70s?

3 PEOPLE: Who was the first English woman to qualify in medicine?

4 INVENTIONS: What is a radiogram?

5 HISTORY: Who was assassinated by John Wilkes Booth?

6 SPORT: How many blank tiles are there in Scrabble?

7 MUSIC: Whose music was used in the film *Death In Venice*?

8 SCIENCE: What took place on a Chicago squash court in 1941?

9 THE ARTS: What was the name of Sherlock Holmes' brother?

10 FILM, TV & RADIO: Which fictitious private detective solved cases over the air on a local radio station?

11 NATURAL HISTORY: What is a more common name for the 'tooth-walking sea horse'?

12 MISCELLANY: What are dim sum?

▶ QUIZMASTER: What are billiard, bulldog, zulu and meershaum varieties of?

TRIVIA QUIZ 12

1 MISCELLANY: Why is her 21st day the 'key-to-the-door' in the life of a worker bee?

2 GEOGRAPHY & TRAVEL: Which state is furthest west: Oregon, North Dakota, Michigan?

3 PEOPLE: What is the most common surname in the world?

4 INVENTIONS: What was the first British car designed to bring motoring to the masses?

5 HISTORY: What nationality was St Patrick?

6 SPORT: What root vegetable grows to the size of a cricket ball and tastes like a cross between a turnip and a cabbage?

7 MUSIC: Mad King Ludwig of Bavaria was obsessed with which composer?

8 SCIENCE: How long, to the nearest 30 seconds, does it take for light to travel from the Sun to the Earth?

9 THE ARTS: How many lines are there in a sonnet?

10 FILM, TV & RADIO: What were Roy Plomley's castaways allowed on their desert island, apart from the Bible and Shakespeare?

11 NATURAL HISTORY: Which mammal lives at the greatest heights?

12 MISCELLANY: What are the following: newtown pippin, russet, bramley?

▶ QUIZMASTER: Which 19th century artist kept and drew wombats?

ANSWERS 11

1 P.G. Wodehouse.

2 South Korea.

3 Elizabeth Garrett Anderson.

4 A radio and gramophone combined.

5 Abraham Lincoln.

6 Two.

7 Mahler's.

8 The first controlled atomic chain reaction.

9 Mycroft.

10 Eddie Shoestring.

11 Walrus.

12 Chinese snacks served with tea in the morning and early afternoon.

■ Smokers' pipes.

ANSWERS 12

1 She finishes her duties in the hive and goes out to forage for nectar.

2 Oregon.

3 The Chinese name Chang.

4 The Austin 7.

5 English.

6 Kohlrabi.

7 Wagner.

8 Eight minutes and 30 seconds.

9 14.

10 Eight records, a book of their choice and a luxury item.

11 The pika, a rodent which has been found in the Himalayas at heights of 17,500 feet.

12 Types of apples.

■ Dante Gabriel Rossetti.

TRIVIA QUIZ 13

1 **MISCELLANY:** How many pints of milk could be bought for £1 in 1914: 60, 110, 165 or 240?

2 **GEOGRAPHY & TRAVEL:** Which river marks the border of the United States and Mexico?

3 **PEOPLE:** What was Valentina Tereshkova's special achievement?

4 **INVENTIONS:** In computing who or what is a hacker?

5 **HISTORY:** What was Oliver Cromwell's title as ruler?

6 **SPORT:** What ingredient, with brandy and lemon juice, completes a sidecar cocktail?

7 **MUSIC:** By what name is Virginia Wynette Pugh better known?

8 **SCIENCE:** What is the popular name of nitrous oxide?

9 **THE ARTS:** The proceeds from which play still finance a London hospital for children?

10 **FILM, TV & RADIO:** Who played the Sorcerer's Apprentice in *Fantasia?*

11 **NATURAL HISTORY:** What tree was used for making longbows?

12 **MISCELLANY:** Which Greek philosopher showed his contempt for materialism by living in a tub?

▶ **QUIZMASTER:** What is Odeon an acronym for?

TRIVIA QUIZ 14

1 **MISCELLANY:** What is the cheapest ingredient of a soufflé and essential if it is to rise?

2 **GEOGRAPHY & TRAVEL:** In which British town or city is there a Bridge Of Sighs?

3 **PEOPLE:** Who was the leader of the Liberal Party before David Steel?

4 **INVENTIONS:** What is the significance to the Rubik Cube of the number 43,252,003,274,489,856,000?

5 **HISTORY:** By what name was Vladimir Ilyich Ulyanov better known?

6 **SPORT:** On what would you perform a randolph?

7 **MUSIC:** Who wrote a piano piece inspired by Hartmann's painting of the witch Baba-Yaga's hut?

8 **SCIENCE:** Which 16-year-old was turned down when he applied for admission to the Swiss Federal Polytechnic Institute?

9 **THE ARTS:** Which playwright was Charlie Chaplin's father-in-law?

10 **FILM, TV & RADIO:** Who turned down an offer to appear in *Flashdance*, which included one per cent of the estimated £50 million takings?

11 **NATURAL HISTORY:** Where did japonica originate?

12 **MISCELLANY:** What do birds use their feathers for, apart from flying and keeping warm?

▶ **QUIZMASTER:** What is the only word in the English language with a double 'i'?

ANSWERS 13

1 240.

2 The Rio Grande.

3 She was the first woman in space.

4 Someone who manipulates other people's computer programmes, usually illegally, to his own advantage.

5 Lord Protector of the Commonwealth.

6 Cointreau.

7 Tammy Wynette.

8 Laughing gas.

9 Peter Pan.

10 Mickey Mouse.

11 The common yew, which was planted in village churchyards for the purpose.

12 Diogenes.

■ Oscar Deutsch entertains our nation.

ANSWERS 14

1 Air.

2 Cambridge.

3 Jeremy Thorpe.

4 It's the number of possible configurations.

5 Lenin.

6 A trampoline.

7 Modest Mussorgsky.

8 Albert Einstein.

9 Eugene O'Neill.

10 Bob Geldof.

11 Japan.

12 Communicating.

■ Skiing.

TRIVIA QUIZ 15

1 MISCELLANY: What are T'ang, Ch'ing and Ming?

2 GEOGRAPHY & TRAVEL: What is Israel's most valuable export?

3 PEOPLE: What is the name of the Queen's youngest son?

4 INVENTIONS: Which of these is the most energy efficient: a swift, a leopard, a man riding a bicycle?

5 HISTORY: What was King George VI's first Christian name?

6 SPORT: Médoc wines are cultivated by which river?

7 MUSIC: Which difficult balletic manoeuvre, carrying the danger of dislocation, was first performed by Marie Taglioni in 1814?

8 SCIENCE: What travels at 741 mph?

9 THE ARTS: Four of Shakespeare's works have a play within a play. Can you name two of them?

10 FILM, TV & RADIO: Who played Rufus T. Firefly in *Duck Soup*?

11 NATURAL HISTORY: Which animal has the most teeth, a cat or a dog?

12 MISCELLANY: What were the 'lolly ladies' of the English Restoration theatres called?

▶ QUIZMASTER: What is the name of the overweight warrior chief of Asterix's tribe?

TRIVIA QUIZ 16

1 MISCELLANY: Fortunes can be seen in it, but in 1785 it cost a fortune itself. What is it?

2 GEOGRAPHY & TRAVEL: In which American city is Hollywood?

3 PEOPLE: What did Louis Blériot do in 1909?

4 INVENTIONS: Spectra 900 is a new material that is light enough to float. How many times stronger than steel is it?

5 HISTORY: Which famous English school had Thomas Arnold as headmaster?

6 SPORT: Where was the first FA Cup Final held?

7 MUSIC: What produce did Molly Malone sell?

8 SCIENCE: If a man tosses a coin and gets heads three times, what are the odds of getting heads the next time?

9 THE ARTS: Who wrote just one novel, called *Savrola*?

10 FILM, TV & RADIO: What is the better known name of elegant dancing star Tula Finklea?

11 NATURAL HISTORY: Are there any wild lions outside Africa?

12 MISCELLANY: How long is a millenium?

▶ QUIZMASTER: Which valuable material has exactly the same atoms as coal?

ANSWERS 15

1 Chinese dynasties.

2 Cut diamonds.

3 Edward.

4 A man riding a bicycle.

5 Albert.

6 The Gironde.

7 Dancing on the pointe (tip-toes).

8 Sound.

9 *Hamlet, A Midsummer Night's Dream, Love's Labour's Lost*, and *The Taming of the Shrew.*

10 Groucho Marx.

11 A dog.

12 Orange girls (Nell Gwynne began her career as one).

■ Vitalstatistix.

ANSWERS 16

1 Tea.

2 Los Angeles.

3 He flew across the English Channel.

4 10.

5 Rugby.

6 Kennington Oval.

7 Cockles and mussels.

8 One in two. The odds are unaffected by previous events.

9 Winston Churchill.

10 Cyd Charisse.

11 Yes. Some Asian lions live wild in India's Gir Reserve.

12 1,000 years.

■ Diamond.

TRIVIA QUIZ 17

▶

1 MISCELLANY: What do mothers Anna Ford, Ursula Andress, Esther Rantzen, Jan Leeming, Joan Collins and Sophia Loren have in common?

2 GEOGRAPHY & TRAVEL: What is the name of the northern light phenomenon caused by charged solar particles striking the earth's atmosphere?

3 PEOPLE: Where is the seat of the Marquess of Bath?

4 INVENTIONS: What was the Bristol Brabazon?

5 HISTORY: Which British monarch had the shortest reign?

6 SPORT: The midget and the rentpayer are varieties of which vegetable?

7 MUSIC: Who saw Mommy kissing Santa Claus in 1953?

8 SCIENCE: What unit measures the loudness of sound?

9 THE ARTS: Which impressionist painter once worked as a teacher in Ramsgate?

10 FILM, TV & RADIO: Where in *The Wizard of Oz* does the Yellow Brick Road go?

11 NATURAL HISTORY: What is the world's fastest land animal?

12 MISCELLANY: Which composer was so anti-semitic he would only conduct Mendelssohn's music if he was wearing gloves?

▶ **QUIZMASTER:** Who or what ate a duck, but was outwitted by a bird, a cat, a small boy and his grandfather?

TRIVIA QUIZ 18

▶

1 MISCELLANY: What do Colley Cibber, John Masefield and John Betjeman have in common?

2 GEOGRAPHY & TRAVEL: What is the capital of South Korea?

3 PEOPLE: Which organisation has the motto 'For home and country'?

4 INVENTIONS: Which car manufacturer commands the largest slice of the British market?

5 HISTORY: Who was the founder of Methodism?

6 SPORT : Which two kicks in football must be played forward?

7 MUSIC: Which group was formed by friends at Charterhouse school?

8 SCIENCE: Who was the first person to win two Nobel Prizes?

9 THE ARTS: Which novelist was exiled to the Channel Islands?

10 FILM, TV & RADIO: Which TV current affairs presenter also owns a chain of local newspapers?

11 NATURAL HISTORY: What is the name of the largest pearl ever found, which had a circumference of four and a half inches and weighed nearly three ounces?

12 MISCELLANY: How many squares are there in a noughts and crosses grid?

▶ **QUIZMASTER:** What is a caryatid?

ANSWERS 17

1 They all had their first child in their late 30s or early 40s.

2 The aurora borealis.

3 Longleat.

4 At one stage, the world's largest airliner, though it was a failure and was scrapped in 1942 after only one had been completed.

5 Lady Jane Grey (nine days).

6 The broad bean.

7 A lot of people! Any of these are correct: The Beverley Sisters, Jimmy Boyd, Billy Cotton and his Band.

8 The decibel.

9 Van Gogh.

10 The Emerald City.

11 The cheetah (capable of speeds of around 70 mph).

12 Wagner.

■ The Wolf in Prokofiev's *Peter And The Wolf*.

ANSWERS 18

1 They were all Poets Laureate.

2 Seoul.

3 The Women's Institute.

4 Ford, with 26.1 per cent of the market in mid-1985.

5 John Wesley.

6 The penalty kick and the kick-off.

7 Genesis.

8 Marie Curie (one for physics and one for chemistry).

9 Victor Hugo.

10 David Dimbleby.

11 The Hope Pearl.

12 One.

■ The correct name for a pillar carved in human form, used to support a roof or doorway.

TRIVIA QUIZ 19

1 MISCELLANY: What connection have Sally Lunns, Madeleines and parkin?

2 GEOGRAPHY & TRAVEL: Which nations are separated by the Bering Strait?

3 PEOPLE: Who called Russia, 'a puzzle within a mystery, wrapped up in an enigma'?

4 INVENTIONS: Why were pneumatic tyres always bursting when they were first introduced?

5 HISTORY: Who was the last Tudor monarch?

6 SPORT: What cheese comes from the caves of Causses, France?

7 MUSIC: Who earned $50 playing harmonica on a Harry Belafonte album in 1960?

8 SCIENCE: Which metal is used for the element in an electric lamp?

9 THE ARTS: Which famous adventure was based on the real-life story of Alexander Selkirk?

10 FILM, TV & RADIO: Which popular actress once starred in a barely credible 1967 TV series about a nun who could fly?

11 NATURAL HISTORY: How many teats does a female hyena have?

12 MISCELLANY: Who was crowned Holy Roman Emperor in 800 AD?

▶ QUIZMASTER: How many lions are there on the Queen's coat of arms?

TRIVIA QUIZ 20

1 MISCELLANY: What do you do with a swizzle stick?

2 GEOGRAPHY & TRAVEL: What natural landscape has almost disappeared from the prairie state of Illinois?

3 PEOPLE: What did Graham Sutherland design for the rebuilt Coventry Cathedral?

4 INVENTIONS: What is the medium that can carry 672 telephone calls simultaneously along a fibre optics cable?

5 HISTORY: Which American Civil War general was defeated at Gettysburg in 1863?

6 SPORT: Name four of the ten ways a cricketer can be out.

7 MUSIC: Which bandleader was killed in a plane crash?

8 SCIENCE: Which hang from the ceiling, stalagmites or stalactites?

9 THE ARTS: What was the name of Rochester's house in Jane Eyre?

10 FILM, TV & RADIO: Who made her 1985 screen debut acting in a film with her mother and playing the same part?

11 NATURAL HISTORY: What is the most dangerous shark?

12 MISCELLANY: Which best-selling author had already made and lost a million pound fortune in the food business before he ever started writing?

▶ QUIZMASTER: London's famous red double decker buses are painted with which other colour running in a horizontal stripe round the middle?

ANSWERS 19

1 They are all cakes.

2 The USA and the USSR.

3 Winston Churchill.

4 Because the recommended air pressure was extremely high.

5 Elizabeth I.

6 Roquefort.

7 Bob Dylan.

8 Tungsten.

9 *Robinson Crusoe*.

10 Sally Field (*The Flying Nun*).

11 Two.

12 Charlemagne.

■ Eight or nine (there is sometimes an optional lion sitting on top of the crown).

ANSWERS 20

1 Stir a drink.

2 Prairie.

3 The altar tapestry.

4 Light.

5 Robert E. Lee.

6 Bowled, LBW, caught, stumped, timed out, run out, handling the ball, obstructing the field, hitting the wicket, or hitting the ball twice.

7 Glenn Miller.

8 Stalactites.

9 Thornfield Hall.

10 Joely Richardson. She and her mother, Vanessa Redgrave, played Jean Travers at different stages of her life in *Wetherby*.

11 The great white shark.

12 Harold Robbins.

■ Cream.

TRIVIA QUIZ 21

1 MISCELLANY: Which novelist explained how the rhinoceros got his skin, the camel his hump and the leopard his spots?

2 GEOGRAPHY & TRAVEL: Where is Casablanca?

3 PEOPLE: What was the Queen Mother's maiden name?

4 INVENTIONS: In which country was table tennis invented?

5 HISTORY: Who was the girl who helped Bonnie Prince Charlie escape to the Isle of Skye?

6 SPORT: All the original Football League Division One teams are still in existence except one. Which one?

7 MUSIC: Who set the World War I poems of Wilfred Owen to music?

8 SCIENCE: What heavenly movement did Copernicus (1473-1543) establish?

9 THE ARTS: What was Jane Austen's first published novel?

10 FILM, TV & RADIO: Which actor played the first Dr Who?

11 NATURAL HISTORY: What kind of creature is the coelacanth, once thought to have been extinct, but which made a come-back in 1938?

12 MISCELLANY: What is a merman?

▶ QUIZMASTER: Who gyred and gimbled in the wabe?

TRIVIA QUIZ 22

1 MISCELLANY: At what stage in a meal would you serve potage?

2 GEOGRAPHY & TRAVEL: What language does an estimated 25% of the population of Los Angeles speak?

3 PEOPLE: Where would you find Black Rod?

4 INVENTIONS: What was the first London street to be lit by gas lamps, in 1807?

5 HISTORY: What was the world's first breakfast cereal sold commercially?

6 SPORT: Latour is first division, Montrose second division and Palmer third division. What are the divisions?

7 MUSIC: What was the first top 30 hit by the Rolling Stones?

8 SCIENCE: Why might tea taste bad at the top of Mount Everest?

9 THE ARTS: Who was the famous first editor of the *New Yorker*?

10 FILM, TV & RADIO: Which actor said the line: 'When you're slapped, you'll take it and like it!'?

11 NATURAL HISTORY: What is the difference between the Manchurian tiger and the Siberian Tiger?

12 MISCELLANY: Virago is the name of a publisher of feminist books, but what does the word virago actually mean?

▶ QUIZMASTER: How many times a year does the average Briton go to the cinema?

ANSWERS 21

1 Rudyard Kipling (in his *Just So Stories*).

2 Morocco.

3 Bowes-Lyon.

4 England.

5 Flora MacDonald.

6 Accrington Stanley.

7 Benjamin Britten (for his *War Requiem*).

8 That the Earth goes round the Sun.

9 *Sense and Sensibility*.

10 William Hartnell.

11 A fish.

12 The male equivalent of a mermaid.

■ The slithy toves (in *Alice Through the Looking Glass*).

ANSWERS 22

1 To start: it is another name for soup.

2 Spanish.

3 The House Of Lords.

4 Pall Mall.

5 Shredded wheat.

6 The 'cru' classifications of Bordeaux wines.

7 'Come On' (July 1963).

8 Because of the altitude, water boils at only 74 degrees centigrade – not a high enough temperature to draw flavour from the tea leaves.

9 Harold Ross.

10 Humphrey Bogart (as Sam Spade in *The Maltese Falcon*).

11 None. They are different names for the same animal.

12 A loud, violent and bad-tempered woman.

■ Once.

TRIVIA QUIZ 23

1 MISCELLANY: What was the most significant world event of August 6, 1945?

2 GEOGRAPHY & TRAVEL: Which London Street, identifiable by its name, was inhabited by a French community in the 16th century?

3 PEOPLE: What is the main Japanese religion?

4 INVENTIONS: Which familiar feature of underground stations first appeared in 1894 as a joy-ride at Coney Island, New York?

5 HISTORY: What was 'Capability' Brown's first given name?

6 SPORT: What is scuba an acronym for?

7 MUSIC: Which hymn first appeared in Holst's *Planet Suite*?

8 SCIENCE: What is the largest planet?

9 THE ARTS: Which French novelist also played goalkeeper for the Algerian football team?

10 FILM, TV & RADIO: What is the name of Dr Who's time machine?

11 NATURAL HISTORY: Do jaguars live wild in the United States?

12 MISCELLANY: What was unusual about the 1985 production of *The Taming Of The Shrew* at the Theatre Royal, Stratford East?

▶ QUIZMASTER: What unexpected event stopped play in the FA Cup Final (Charlton v. Burnley) of 1947?

TRIVIA QUIZ 24

1 MISCELLANY: Which fabulous monster, half bull and half man, lived in a labyrinth in Crete?

2 GEOGRAPHY & TRAVEL: Of the three main Japanese islands, Kyushu, Honshu and Hokkaido, which lies furthest north?

3 PEOPLE: Which politician was known as the Welsh wizard?

4 INVENTIONS: What unit of weight measurement derives from the carob seed?

5 HISTORY: Who introduced the printing press in England in 1476?

6 SPORT: Who was the last European to win the World Heavyweight Boxing title?

7 MUSIC: Which composer wrote a quintet to a fish?

8 SCIENCE: Why do soap bubbles rise when blown from a bubble pipe?

9 THE ARTS: What was Shakespeare's last play?

10 FILM, TV & RADIO: From which TV quiz show does the catchphrase 'Bernie the bolt' come?

11 NATURAL HISTORY: What is the oldest living thing?

12 MISCELLANY: Who wrote *A Boring Story*?

▶ QUIZMASTER: Is every member of a circus' audience contubernial?

ANSWERS 23

1 An atomic bomb was dropped on Hiroshima.

2 Petty France.

3 Shinto.

4 The escalator.

5 Lancelot.

6 Self-contained underwater breathing apparatus.

7 'I Vow To Thee My Country'.

8 Jupiter (318 times the mass of the Earth).

9 Albert Camus.

10 The Tardis.

11 No (they were last seen in the 1940s).

12 It had an all-woman cast.

■ The ball burst.

ANSWERS 24

1 The Minotaur.

2 Hokkaido.

3 David Lloyd George.

4 The carat.

5 William Caxton.

6 Ingemar Johannsen.

7 Franz Schubert (*The Trout Quintet* in A Major).

8 Because the air from your lungs is warmer, and therefore lighter, than the surrounding air.

9 *The Tempest.*

10 *The Golden Shot.*

11 The bristlecone pine tree (one in Nevada is estimated to be 4,900 years old).

12 Anton Chekhov.

■ Yes (it means they occupy the same tent).

TRIVIA QUIZ 25

1 MISCELLANY: What marathon procession hit the headlines in 1936?

2 GEOGRAPHY & TRAVEL: What did France, West Germany, Belgium, Luxembourg, Holland and Italy sign in 1958?

3 PEOPLE: Where is the headquarters of the United Nations?

4 INVENTIONS: What is the nickname of the sub-machine gun co-invented by General J.T. Thompson?

5 HISTORY: Which U.S. President brought in prohibition in 1919?

6 SPORT: Who won the 1960 Olympic marathon without shoes?

7 MUSIC: Who wrote the words to the popular Victorian ballad 'Come Into The Garden Maud'?

8 SCIENCE: Who introduced the terms negative and positive in relation to electricity?

9 THE ARTS: From which bridge was Wordsworth enjoying the view when he said 'Earth has not anything to show more fair'?

10 FILM, TV & RADIO: Which *Blue Peter* presenter had a dog called Shep?

11 NATURAL HISTORY: What living asterisk moves at 15 centimetres a minute?

12 MISCELLANY: The battle of Austerlitz was fought in Moravia. In which modern country is it?

▶ **QUIZMASTER:** There are 26 letters in the alphabet and 2,598 pages in the Shorter Oxford English Dictionary. How many pages, to the nearest 10, consist of words beginning with K?

TRIVIA QUIZ 26

1 MISCELLANY: What was the profession of Andrea Palladio?

2 GEOGRAPHY & TRAVEL: Which is the world's busiest international airport?

3 PEOPLE: Who was the first footballer to be knighted?

4 INVENTIONS: What is a trimaran?

5 HISTORY: Who said 'I find no fault in this man'?

6 SPORT: What do you call the technique of partly baking a flan case before filling it?

7 MUSIC: What colour is Max Headroom's hair?

8 SCIENCE: What was the great discovery of William Harvey?

9 THE ARTS: Who painted a portrait of Winston Churchill that was loathed by its subject and later destroyed by his family?

10 FILM, TV & RADIO: Who said 'When I was nine I played the Demon King in Cinderella and it launched me on a long and happy life of being a monster'?

11 NATURAL HISTORY: Lizards shed their skin by peeling. Do mammals shed their skin?

12 MISCELLANY: What is the third dimension?

▶ **QUIZMASTER:** What is a one-legged camera support called?

ANSWERS 25

1 The Jarrow march.

2 The Treaty of Rome.

3 New York.

4 Tommy gun.

5 Woodrow Wilson.

6 Abebe Bikila.

7 Tennyson.

8 Benjamin Franklin.

9 Westminster Bridge.

10 John Noakes.

11 The Starfish.

12 Czechoslovakia.

■ 19.

ANSWERS 26

1 Architecture.

2 Heathrow (29 million passengers a year).

3 Sir Stanley Matthews.

4 A boat with three hulls.

5 Pontius Pilate.

6 Baking blind.

7 Blond.

8 That blood circulates round the body.

9 Graham Sutherland.

10 Boris Karloff.

11 Yes, most do. (Humans change their skin every six months as the dead cells flake off.)

12 Depth.

■ A unipod.

TRIVIA QUIZ 27

1 MISCELLANY: What is the term for the course of training nearly 5,000 potential taxi drivers undergo annually in London?

2 GEOGRAPHY & TRAVEL: What single desert contains half the desert surface of the world?

3 PEOPLE: What is the deciding qualification of a true Cockney?

4 INVENTIONS: What happened on the R100's maiden flight?

5 HISTORY: For which British monarch was the gold coronation coach made?

6 SPORT: The name of which game is Latin for 'I play'?

7 MUSIC: Which opera was commissioned by the Khedive of Egypt?

8 SCIENCE: In which monarch's reign was the word 'electricity' first used?

9 THE ARTS: Who said, 'A thing of beauty is a joy forever'?

10 FILM, TV & RADIO: Which radio play starts with the words, "To begin at the beginning: it is spring, moonless night in the small town, starless and bible black'?

11 NATURAL HISTORY: What fish-eating bird of prey has recently re-established itself in Scotland?

12 MISCELLANY: How many people, to the nearest thousand, does Heathrow Airport employ?

▶ QUIZMASTER: Who painted a reproduction of *The Last Supper* on the wall of his house and covered it with wallpaper as a surprise for next owners?

TRIVIA QUIZ 28

1 MISCELLANY: Which London art gallery caused a furore by exhibiting a pile of bricks?

2 GEOGRAPHY & TRAVEL: What is the name of New York's main airport?

3 PEOPLE: What was the nickname of the German fighter pilot Baron von Richthofen?

4 INVENTIONS: What are the trails left in the sky by aircraft composed of?

5 HISTORY: Who was the first Archbishop of Canterbury?

6 SPORT: Which poet played cricket for Harrow against Eton in 1805?

7 MUSIC: What does ZTT stand for?

8 SCIENCE: In navigation, what measures 1.8 metres?

9 THE ARTS: Who was Dan Dare's evil adversary?

10 FILM, TV & RADIO: Which Disney character became an agent for Timothy Mouse?

11 NATURAL HISTORY: Why do crocodiles swallow stones?

12 MISCELLANY: Lady's delight is more commonly called what?

▶ QUIZMASTER: Where would you find the Akond of Swat?

ANSWERS 27

1 The Knowledge.

2 The Sahara.

3 To be born within the sound of Bow bells.

4 It flew to Canada and back. (It was the R101 airship which crashed.)

5 George III.

6 Ludo.

7 Verdi's *Aida*.

8 Elizabeth I. (The word was first used by William Gilbert).

9 John Keats.

10 Dylan Thomas' *Under Milk Wood*.

11 The osprey (there are now about 20 pairs).

12 45,000.

■ Ralph Steadman.

ANSWERS 28

1 The Tate.

2 Kennedy Airport.

3 The Red Baron.

4 Condensed water vapour.

5 Saint Augustine.

6 Byron.

7 Zang Tuum Tumb.

8 A fathom.

9 The Mekon.

10 Dumbo the Elephant.

11 To act as stabilisers when swimming.

12 The violet.

■ In a nonsense poem by Edward Lear.

TRIVIA QUIZ 29

1 **MISCELLANY:** What percentage of British adults, to the nearest 10%, drink alcohol?

2 **GEOGRAPHY & TRAVEL:** What is the world's driest desert?

3 **PEOPLE:** What is the 'Fourth Estate'?

4 **INVENTIONS:** What is the term used to describe sound waves outside the audible range?

5 **HISTORY:** What nationality was Pocohontas?

6 **SPORT:** Who scored most runs in his first Test Match?

7 **MUSIC:** *Lilac Time* is a film which tells the life story and uses the music of which composer?

8 **SCIENCE:** Which medical pioneer taught his students under the shade of a plane tree on the island of Cos?

9 **THE ARTS:** Which author edited *Household Words*?

10 **FILM, TV & RADIO:** Which series, when shown in Germany, resulted in floods of 'confession' calls from viewers?

11 **NATURAL HISTORY:** In what way is the behaviour of honeysuckle and bindweed exactly opposite when climbing upwards?

12 **MISCELLANY:** Who first said: 'There's a sucker born every minute'?

▶ **QUIZMASTER:** Why do gardeners plant milk bottles in lawns?

TRIVIA QUIZ 30

1 **MISCELLANY:** who wrote an ode to the railway bridge over the Tay and a lament when it collapsed?

2 **GEOGRAPHY & TRAVEL:** Which country inspired the English word serendipity, meaning 'unexpected delight'?

3 **PEOPLE:** Who turned the word 'walkies!' into a command?

4 **INVENTIONS:** Which is the 'trailing edge' of an aircraft wing?

5 **HISTORY:** Which English king was killed at the Battle of Hastings?

6 **SPORT:** Two founder members of the Second Division were known as Ardwick and Small Heath. What are they now called?

7 **MUSIC:** What coalition brought a new version of a Donna Summer No. 1 into the charts in 1985?

8 **SCIENCE:** Why does a pendulum clock run slower in hot weather?

9 **THE ARTS:** Which English novelist and playwright was once a full-time cinema critic?

10 **FILM, TV & RADIO:** What favourite expression of John Wayne in the 1956 film *The Searchers* also appeared in Buddy Holly And The Crickets' first hit?

11 **NATURAL HISTORY:** How long does it take an orchid to grow from seed?

12 **MISCELLANY:** Which six-letter word contains no vowels?

▶ **QUIZMASTER:** Who said: 'If you can lie on the floor without holding on you're not really drunk'?

1 90%

2 The Atacama desert, Chile (one town has never recorded rain).

3 The press.

4 Ultrasonic.

5 She was an American Indian.

6 Lawrence Rowe of the West Indies, who scored 214 and 100 not out.

7 Franz Schubert.

8 Hippocrates.

9 Charles Dickens.

10 *Holocaust*.

11 Honeysuckle spirals clockwise and bindweed spirals anti-clockwise.

12 Circus impresario Phineas T. Barnum.

■ The sound of the wind across the tops frightens moles away.

ANSWERS 30

1 William McGonagall.

2 Sri Lanka.

3 Barbara Woodhouse.

4 The rear edge.

5 Harold.

6 Manchester City and Birmingham City.

7 Bronski Beat with Marc Almond.

8 Because the pendulum expands in length and swings slower.

9 Graham Greene.

10 'That'll be the day'.

11 Eight years.

12 Rhythm.

■ Dean Martin.

TRIVIA QUIZ 31

1 MISCELLANY: Which vegetable relative of the cauliflower do we know by its Italian name?

2 GEOGRAPHY & TRAVEL: What lake was the Victorian Sir Richard Burton the first to discover in Tanganyika?

3 PEOPLE: Who performed the first heart transplant?

4 INVENTIONS: In electrical wiring, how do flex and cable differ?

5 HISTORY: Which general was killed at the seige of Khartoum in 1885?

6 SPORT: Which part of the pig is used for ham?

7 MUSIC: Which Gilbert and Sullivan opera is sub-titled Bunthorne's Bride?

8 SCIENCE: Which scientist was born so prematurely his mother said he could have been put in a quart mug?

9 THE ARTS: Which family lived at Brideshead?

10 FILM, TV & RADIO: Name one of the actresses who play Mrs Slocombe and Miss Brahms in the ladies' underwear department of Grace Brothers' Store.

11 NATURAL HISTORY: How large can a giant clam grow: three inches across; 18 inches; three feet; five feet?

12 MISCELLANY: What is the term for the driver of a team of huskies?

▶ QUIZMASTER: Which country uses the markka as currency?

TRIVIA QUIZ 32

1 MISCELLANY: Why was Hiroo Onoda greeted home to Japan as a war hero in 1974?

2 GEOGRAPHY & TRAVEL: What happened on the Hawaiian island of Oahu on December 7, 1941?

3 PEOPLE: How many single-parent families are there in Britain: one million, half a million, 200,000?

4 INVENTIONS: What is Nyoil?

5 HISTORY: How did Nurse Edith Cavell die in 1915?

6 SPORT: What was the first non-English club to win the FA cup?

7 MUSIC: What band have the following all performed in at one time or another: Ginger Baker, Mick Jagger, Eric Burdon, Paul Jones and Danny Thompson?

8 SCIENCE: What does the mnemonic 'run off you girls, boys in view' tell us?

9 THE ARTS: Which angry young man wrote: *Epitaph For George Dillon?*

10 FILM, TV & RADIO: Which is the longest-running TV quiz show?

11 NATURAL HISTORY: What does the Colorado Whip-poor-will do that distinguishes it from every other kind of bird?

12 MISCELLANY: What remained closed for 3,000 years until February 1923?

▶ QUIZMASTER: Where are Eriador, Rhûn, Gondor and the Bay Of Belfalas?

ANSWERS 31

1 Broccoli.

2 Lake Tanganyika.

3 Professor Christian Barnard.

4 Flex contains many fine strands of wire, cable has relatively few.

5 General Gordon.

6 The top of the hind legs.

7 *Patience.*

8 Isaac Newton.

9 The Marchmains.

10 Molly Sugden and Wendy Richard.

11 Five feet.

12 A musher.

■ Finland

ANSWERS 32

1 He had been carrying on World War II single-handedly on a remote Philippine island.

2 The Japanese bombed the American Pacific Fleet at Pearl Harbor.

3 One million.

4 Nylon impregnated with oil.

5 She was shot by the Germans.

6 Cardiff City in 1927.

7 Alexis Korner's Blues Incorporated.

8 The sequence of colours in the rainbow: red, orange, yellow, green, blue, indigo and violet.

9 John Osborne.

10 *University Challenge* (which has run since 1962).

11 It hibernates in winter.

12 The tomb of Tutankhamun.

■ In Middle Earth (the land Tolkein created in *Lord Of The Rings*).

TRIVIA QUIZ 33

1 MISCELLANY: What are 'ringers' and 'jillaroos'?

2 GEOGRAPHY & TRAVEL: In which country is Ho Chi Minh City?

3 PEOPLE: What is the name of the Cardinal Archbishop of Westminster?

4 INVENTIONS: What kind of internal-combustion engine works on the principle of a rotating triangular shaft?

5 HISTORY: Which royal residence on the Isle of Wight now belongs to the nation?

6 SPORT: How many tiles are there in a domino set?

7 MUSIC: Which Scottish singer married a German Hare Krishna devotee?

8 SCIENCE: What metal do we get from hematite ore?

9 THE ARTS: Which fictitious character lives at Bywater Street, Chelsea?

10 FILM, TV & RADIO: Who is the only actor to have received a posthumous Oscar?

11 NATURAL HISTORY: A sea wasp can kill a human in less than a minute. What sort of animal or fish is it?

12 MISCELLANY: In which country did Arthur C. Clarke make his home?

▶ QUIZMASTER: What reference book, published in 1852, classified words for the first time according to the ideas they expressed?

TRIVIA QUIZ 34

1 MISCELLANY: The prairie dog is a member of what order of animals?

2 GEOGRAPHY & TRAVEL: Where is the Gulf of Carpentaria?

3 PEOPLE: What is a recidivist?

4 INVENTIONS: Which car, introduced in 1907, required 48 feet to stop from a speed of 25 mph?

5 HISTORY: What did the Franks Commission report on?

6 SPORT: If you were turning meat into a daube, what would you be doing with it?

7 MUSIC: What was the Beatles' first record on the Apple label?

8 SCIENCE: What is a white dwarf?

9 THE ARTS: What long-suffering teenager was created by Sue Townsend?

10 FILM, TV & RADIO: In which serial would you find Mr Legge, Miss Booth and Mrs Wallace?

11 NATURAL HISTORY: Snails have no jaws or teeth. How do they eat?

12 MISCELLANY: Who promised his customers 'any colour so long as it's black'?

▶ QUIZMASTER: What was created by James I in 1606 as a symbolic means of uniting England and Scotland, but was disliked by both nations?

ANSWERS 33

1 Australian cowboys and cowgirls.

2 Vietnam.

3 Basil Hume.

4 The Wankel engine.

5 Osborne.

6 28.

7 Annie Lennox.

8 Iron.

9 George Smiley in the Le Carré novels.

10 Peter Finch.

11 A jellyfish.

12 Sri Lanka.

■ Roget's *Thesaurus*.

ANSWERS 34

1 Rodent.

2 Australia.

3 Someone who relapses into crime.

4 The Rolls-Royce Silver Ghost.

5 The Falklands War.

6 Braising it gently and adding herbs.

7 'Hey Jude'

8 A dense star, usually near the end of its life, that has shrunk to the size of a planet.

9 Adrian Mole.

10 *Grange Hill*.

11 They file their food down with a rasping tongue.

12 Henry Ford.

■ The Union Jack.

TRIVIA QUIZ 35

1 MISCELLANY: What is the name of the oil reservoir at the bottom of a crank-case?

2 GEOGRAPHY & TRAVEL: Which American state is bordered by Colorado, Arizona, Nevada, Wyoming and Idaho?

3 PEOPLE: Who made the first solo trans-Atlantic flight?

4 INVENTIONS: What is xerography?

5 HISTORY: Who built Hampton Court?

6 SPORT: Which Olympic event did Mary Peters win in 1972?

7 MUSIC: Which opera's cast list includes an owl, a woodpecker, a gnat, a badger, a jay, a frog, a grasshopper and a fox?

8 SCIENCE: Who introduced the idea that electrons move round the nuclei of atoms in well defined orbits?

9 THE ARTS: Who fell through the ice at Dingley Dell?

10 FILM, TV & RADIO: What is the name of the Cannon ranch?

11 NATURAL HISTORY: Are sea snakes poisonous?

12 MISCELLANY: Who was Chancellor of the Exchequer when Britain returned to the gold standard?

▶ QUIZMASTER: Why is there a theory that Napoleon died by poisoning when he was imprisoned on St Helena?

TRIVIA QUIZ 36

1 MISCELLANY: What is your star sign if you are born on May 30?

2 GEOGRAPHY & TRAVEL: What object, later named Eureka, was found by children in the dust at Hopetown, South Africa in 1866?

3 PEOPLE: What would you be doing if you were the 'first foot'?

4 INVENTIONS: What, in sound reproduction, is the name of a slow fluctuation in pitch?

5 HISTORY: By what nickname was George Brummell usually known?

6 SPORT: Which driver won the British Grand Prix four years running, from 1962 to 1965?

7 MUSIC: Who produced *Sergeant Pepper's Lonely Hearts Club Band*?

8 SCIENCE: Why do you feel cold in wet clothes?

9 THE ARTS: What was Paul Scott's sequel to the 'Raj Quartet'?

10 FILM, TV & RADIO: What instrument did Gene Hackman play in *The Conversation*?

11 NATURAL HISTORY: Is the skin of freshwater fish waterproof?

12 MISCELLANY: Who was the first known person reputed to have been born by Caesarian section?

▶ QUIZMASTER: What did Sir Thomas Blanket first manufacture in 1340?

ANSWERS 35

1 The sump.

2 Utah.

3 Charles Lindbergh.

4 The photo-copying process.

5 Cardinal Wolsey.

6 The women's pentathlon.

7 *The Cunning Little Vixen* by Janaček.

8 Niels Bohr.

9 Mr Pickwick.

10 The High Chaparral.

11 Yes. The 50 known types of sea snake are venomous.

12 Winston Churchill.

■ Because the paint on the walls of the house where he was confined on the island of St Helena contained arsenic.

ANSWERS 36

1 Gemini.

2 The country's first diamond.

3 You would be the first visitor after midnight on New Year's Eve.

4 A wow.

5 He was Beau Brummell.

6 Jim Clark.

7 George Martin.

8 As the moisture evaporates it takes heat from the skin.

9 *Staying On.*

10 The saxophone.

11 No, they get moisture through their skin.

12 Julius Caesar.

■ Blankets.

TRIVIA QUIZ 37

1 MISCELLANY: What did Colonel Thomas Blood try to steal in 1675?

2 GEOGRAPHY & TRAVEL: What country is the home of Flemings and Walloons?

3 PEOPLE: Who is known as the 'First Lady'?

4 INVENTIONS: What two products did Frederich Albrecht Winzer extract in one process from coal?

5 HISTORY: In what year was the wearing of front seat belts in Britain made compulsory?

6 SPORT: What is the Japanese art of miniature tree cultivation called?

7 MUSIC: Which symphony includes a setting of Schiller's *'Ode To Joy'*?

8 SCIENCE: You cannot see more than 6,000 of them and then only at night. What are they?

9 THE ARTS: What was the name of Sherlock Holmes' landlady?

10 FILM, TV & RADIO: Who plays Dr Leonard Gillespie in *Dr Kildare*?

11 NATURAL HISTORY: Can whales drown?

12 MISCELLANY: Which university is older, Oxford or Cambridge?

▶ QUIZMASTER: Which is older, Barbie or Sindy?

TRIVIA QUIZ 38

1 MISCELLANY: What is a colombophile?

2 GEOGRAPHY & TRAVEL: Which is Britain's tallest cathedral spire?

3 PEOPLE: What was the name of Indira Gandhi's father?

4 INVENTIONS: Where was skiing invented?

5 HISTORY: What pictorial record of the Battle of Hastings was made by women?

6 SPORT: What is another name for a castle in chess?

7 MUSIC: Who owns the Philles label?

8 SCIENCE: What other element, besides hydrogen, is water composed of?

9 THE ARTS: By what name was Lord Greystoke better known?

10 FILM, TV & RADIO: Who starred in *Singing In The Rain* and *Xanadu*?

11 NATURAL HISTORY: Name a British bird smaller than the wren.

12 MISCELLANY: What did medieval artists use to bind their pigment paints?

▶ QUIZMASTER: What is the minimum annual earning requirement for an American Express Gold Card applicant?

ANSWERS 37

1 The Crown Jewels.

2 Belgium.

3 The wife of the American president.

4 Gas and coke.

5 1983.

6 Bonsai.

7 Beethoven's *Ninth Symphony*.

8 Stars.

9 Mrs Hudson.

10 Raymond Massey.

11 Yes (if they have to remain underwater for much longer than one hour).

12 Oxford.

■ In 1985 the Barbie doll is 25, Sindy is 22.

ANSWERS 38

1 A pigeon fancier.

2 Salisbury.

3 Pandit Jawaharlal Nehru.

4 Norway.

5 The Bayeux Tapestry.

6 Rook.

7 Phil Spector.

8 Oxygen.

9 Tarzan.

10 Gene Kelly.

11 The goldcrest and the firecrest are both smaller.

12 Egg yolk.

■ £25,000.

TRIVIA QUIZ 39

1 **MISCELLANY:** Where might you find a ha-ha and a knot?

2 **GEOGRAPHY & TRAVEL:** Which is Africa's most populous nation?

3 **PEOPLE:** Which American said 'I have a dream'?

4 **INVENTIONS:** What does the aviation term V.T.O. stand for?

5 **HISTORY:** Which travellers set sail in *The Mayflower* in 1620?

6 **SPORT:** Which English cricket captain suffered from epilepsy?

7 **MUSIC:** Who first titillated press and public, not so much by his single 'White Boy', but by his looks in 1982?

8 **SCIENCE:** Alfred Wegener claimed all the continents were once part of a single land mass. What did he call it?

9 **THE ARTS:** What have Thomas Keneally, J.M. Coetzee and Anita Brookner all won in the last few years?

10 **FILM, TV & RADIO:** What are the Christian names of Cannon and Ball?

11 **NATURAL HISTORY:** Name one of the two mammals which lay eggs.

12 **MISCELLANY:** What was Thomas Hardy's original profession?

▶ **QUIZMASTER:** What is the Radcliffe Camera?

TRIVIA QUIZ 40

1 **MISCELLANY:** What boundary did Hyde Park Corner mark until the end of the 19th century?

2 **GEOGRAPHY & TRAVEL:** Two countries have names which mean 'Land Of The South'. Can you name one of them?

3 **PEOPLE:** Who competes for the Dunmow Flitch?

4 **INVENTIONS:** What is the source of lanolin?

5 **HISTORY:** Who was the influential monk at the court of Tsar Nicholas II?

6 **SPORT:** Who played for Stoke City in 1931 and for England in 1957?

7 **MUSIC:** Which musical is set round a performance of *The Taming Of The Shrew*?

8 **SCIENCE:** Which is heavier, gold or platinum?

9 **THE ARTS:** Name three of Christopher Robin's animal friends, apart from Pooh.

10 **FILM, TV & RADIO:** Spell the first name of the presenter of *This Is Your Life*.

11 **NATURAL HISTORY:** What berries are commonly used to flavour English gin?

12 **MISCELLANY:** Which municipal appointment did Richard Whittington hold?

▶ **QUIZMASTER:** Which common word has five consecutive vowels?

ANSWERS 39

1 In a garden.

2 Nigeria.

3 Martin Luther King.

4 Vertical take-off.

5 The Pilgrim Fathers.

6 Tony Greig.

7 Boy George.

8 Pangaea.

9 The Booker Prize.

10 Tommy Cannon and Bobby Ball.

11 The duck-billed platypus and the spiny anteater (echidna).

12 Architecture.

■ A library.

ANSWERS 40

1 The London boundary.

2 Vietnam and Australia.

3 Happily married couples.

4 Sheep's wool

5 Rasputin.

6 Stanley Matthews.

7 *Kiss Me Kate* by Cole Porter.

8 Platinum.

9 Tigger, Owl, Eeyore, Piglet, Kanga, Baby Roo and Rabbit.

10 Eamonn.

11 Juniper berries.

12 Lord Mayor of London.

■ Queueing.

TRIVIA QUIZ 41

1 MISCELLANY: What is the name of the Japanese mattress whose design is 4,000 years old?

2 GEOGRAPHY & TRAVEL: In which country do the women of the Padaung wear 20 pounds of brass rings round their necks?

3 PEOPLE: Can British convicts vote in general elections?

4 INVENTIONS: Who invented dynamite?

5 HISTORY: Which famous writer was imprisoned for nearly two years in Reading jail?

6 SPORT: Which West Indian spin bowlers are immortalised in a calypso?

7 MUSIC: Which film soundtrack featured Glenn Frey, Patti Labelle, Shalamar and the Pointer Sisters?

8 SCIENCE: Which nation operates the world's largest optical telescope?

9 THE ARTS: Which book starts with the words '*Marley was dead*'?

10 FILM, TV & RADIO: Which Radio Two presenter once had a No. 1 hit with a single called 'The Man from Laramie'?

11 NATURAL HISTORY: Name one of the three main identifying features of deadly nightshade.

12 MISCELLANY: What do Oswald Fish and the Laird of Abbotsford have in common?

▶ QUIZMASTER: Which machine is the odd one out: Apple, Cherry, Apricot, Philips P5020, Commodore 8032?

TRIVIA QUIZ 42

1 MISCELLANY: What is the correct name for a gazebo on the roof of a house?

2 GEOGRAPHY & TRAVEL: Which province provides 25% of Canada's agricultural income?

3 PEOPLE: What is meant by the 'old boy network'?

4 INVENTIONS: What hi-fi innovation was a spin-off from the ill-fated laser video?

5 HISTORY: Who was the mother of Queen Elizabeth I?

6 SPORT: Who described the 1972 World Chess Championship as, 'The free world against the lying, cheating, hypocritical Russians'?

7 MUSIC: Who said, 'We're more popular than Jesus Christ now'?

8 SCIENCE: What is measured on the Beaufort Scale?

9 THE ARTS: Which English playwright was murdered by his lover in 1967?

10 FILM, TV & RADIO: Who are the Clampetts?

11 NATURAL HISTORY: Which flower's name is a corruption of the French for 'lion's tooth'?

12 MISCELLANY: Why is Fleet Street in London so called?

▶ QUIZMASTER: How many liveried servants, to the nearest ten, did Lord Mountbatten employ at his Delhi residence when he was Viceroy of India?

ANSWERS 41

1 Futon.

2 Burma.

3 No.

4 Alfred Nobel.

5 Oscar Wilde.

6 Ramadhin and Valentino.

7 Beverley Hills Cop.

8 USSR.

9 *A Christmas Carol*.

10 Jimmy Young.

11 Leaves in equal pairs, dull purple flowers, black, cherry-sized berries.

12 They are both characters in A.N. Wilson books.

■ The Cherry is a car; the other four are computers.

ANSWERS 42

1 A belvedere.

2 Saskatchewan.

3 The system by which appointments are given to former pupils of the same small group of public schools or universities.

4 The compact audio disc.

5 Anne Boleyn.

6 Bobbie Fischer (who was playing Boris Spassky).

7 John Lennon.

8 Wind force.

9 Joe Orton.

10 The Beverley Hillbillies.

11 Dandelion (*dent de lion*).

12 The Fleet river, now channelled underground, passes nearby just before it reaches the Thames.

■ Approximately 344.

TRIVIA QUIZ 43

1 MISCELLANY: Who designed the modern stained glass window at The Church Of All Saints, Tudeley, Kent?

2 GEOGRAPHY & TRAVEL: What is the world's second highest mountain?

3 PEOPLE: Who was the first Briton to sail around the world?

4 INVENTIONS: What does black represent in colour-coded household wiring?

5 HISTORY: Which city was first the capital of Wessex, then England?

6 SPORT: What is the name for members of the cabbage family?

7 MUSIC: Who is the son of Scott Young, one of Canada's best-known sports columnists?

8 SCIENCE: Which was discovered first, codeine or aspirin?

9 THE ARTS: Who was the hero of *Diary Of A Nobody*?

10 FILM, TV & RADIO: What TV musical drama, written by Dennis Potter, was named after a 1930s popular song?

11 NATURAL HISTORY: What medical use is made of the foxglove?

12 MISCELLANY: What happened at Golgotha?

QUIZMASTER: What was comprehensive schoolboy William Hague given at a Conservative Party Conference which caused him to hit the headlines?

TRIVIA QUIZ 44

1 MISCELLANY: What was the name of the London society founded by Whig politicians at the time of James II?

2 GEOGRAPHY & TRAVEL: Name two of the four countries which border on Lake Chad.

3 PEOPLE: What does the abbreviation REME stand for?

4 INVENTIONS: The non-stick frying pan was a spin-off from which area of research?

5 HISTORY: Where is Karl Marx buried?

6 SPORT: What is the name of water paint mixed with gum?

7 MUSIC: For which famous ballet company did Stravinsky write *The Firebird*, *Petroushka* and *The Rite of Spring*?

8 SCIENCE: How many people, on average, are killed by lightning in Britain every year?

9 THE ARTS: Which author died on the same day as Shakespeare?

10 FILM, TV & RADIO: Who created Rambling Sid Rumpole?

11 NATURAL HISTORY: What is the smallest British mammal?

12 MISCELLANY: What happened to Attila The Hun on his wedding night?

QUIZMASTER: What type of duck is really a fish?

ANSWERS 43

1 Marc Chagall.

2 K2 (in Pakistan's Karakoram range).

3 Sir Francis Drake.

4 Neutral.

5 Winchester.

6 Brassicas.

7 Neil Young.

8 Codeine was discovered in 1821, aspirin in 1893.

9 Mr Pooter.

10 *Pennies From Heaven*.

11 It is the source of the drug *digitalis*, used to treat heart conditions.

12 Jesus was crucified there.

■ A standing ovation for a speech he made.

ANSWERS 44

1 The Kit-Kat Club.

2 Nigeria, Chad, Niger, Cameroon.

3 Royal Electrical and Mechanical Engineers.

4 Space.

5 Highgate Cemetery, London.

6 Gouache.

7 The Diaghilev.

8 12.

9 Cervantes.

10 Kenneth Williams in *Round The Horne*.

11 The pygmy shrew (sometimes called the lesser shrew).

12 He died through drinking too much wine.

■ Bombay duck.

TRIVIA QUIZ 45

1 MISCELLANY: How long does it take the Earth to travel one and a half million miles?

2 GEOGRAPHY & TRAVEL: In which country is the site of the Battle of Waterloo?

3 PEOPLE: Who reached the South Pole just ahead of Captain Scott?

4 INVENTIONS: What is the underwater equivalent of radar?

5 HISTORY: What is the historical connection between Sandwich, Dover, Hythe, Hastings and Romney?

6 SPORT: Why was the England/Australia Test Match of 1938 at Old Trafford so disappointing?

7 MUSIC: Which Fleetwood Mac album cost $1 million to produce in 1979?

8 SCIENCE: By what slightly less explosive name is methyl-2,4,6-nitrobenzene known?

9 THE ARTS: Which eminent French novelist defended Dreyfus when he was accused of betraying military secrets?

10 FILM, TV & RADIO: Which radio and TV presenter made the hit parade in 1978 with a version of the Cornish Floral Dance?

11 NATURAL HISTORY: What sort of animal lives in a holt?

12 MISCELLANY: Where did Edward III keep his greyhounds?

▶ QUIZMASTER: How did Montravia Kaskarak Hitari, better known as Alfie, distinguish himself in 1983?

TRIVIA QUIZ 46

1 MISCELLANY: In which year was President J.F. Kennedy assassinated?

2 GEOGRAPHY & TRAVEL: What is the capital of Sri Lanka?

3 PEOPLE: What do agrophobics fear?

4 INVENTIONS: With what branch of science do you associate the words bug and bootstrap?

5 HISTORY: Who designed St Paul's Cathedral?

6 SPORT: What fashionable fantasy game is known as D & D?

7 MUSIC: Which popular Irish group has only one letter in its name?

8 SCIENCE: What is a clinophobic scared of?

9 THE ARTS: Which writer's Christian names were Herbert George?

10 FILM, TV & RADIO: Which university uses the radio and TV as its lecture theatre?

11 NATURAL HISTORY: How many legs does a crab have?

12 MISCELLANY: Who now possesses the Koh-i-noor diamond, once owned by the man who built the Taj Mahal, Shah Jahan?

▶ QUIZMASTER: Which of these is the odd one out: cat, storm, needle, banana?

ANSWERS 45

1 24 hours.

2 Belgium.

3 Captain Roald Amundsen.

4 Sonar.

5 They were the original Cinque Ports.

6 It was abandoned before the first ball was bowled.

7 *Tusk.*

8 TNT.

9 Zola.

10 Terry Wogan.

11 The otter.

12 The Isle Of Dogs (hence the name).

■ He was Supreme Champion at Crufts.

ANSWERS 46

1 1963.

2 Colombo.

3 Open spaces.

4 Computer science.

5 Christopher Wren.

6 Dungeons and Dragons.

7 U2.

8 Going to bed.

9 H.G. Wells.

10 The Open University.

11 10.

12 The Queen.

■ The banana doesn't have an eye.

TRIVIA QUIZ 47

1 MISCELLANY: What is the name of Goscinny and Uderzo's menhir delivery man?

2 GEOGRAPHY & TRAVEL: Which city houses the headquarters of the EEC?

3 PEOPLE: Which American statesman won the Nobel Peace Prize in 1973?

4 INVENTIONS: What did Percy Shaw invent and market two years after a foggy drive in 1933?

5 HISTORY: Who was the queen of the Iceni who rode into battle against the Romans?

6 SPORT: Which football club plays at Cold Blow Lane?

7 MUSIC: Name the two groups whose first three singles reached number one in the British charts.

8 SCIENCE: Why was uranium so called?

9 THE ARTS: Who was Biggles' evil German adversary?

10 FILM, TV & RADIO: Which singer did Sissy Spacek portray in 'Coal Miner's Daughter'?

11 NATURAL HISTORY: What is the largest bird after the ostrich?

12 MISCELLANY: Which is the odd one out: Venus, Anadyomene, Juno, Aphrodite?

▶ QUIZMASTER: What is the next number in this series: 1, 1, 2, 3, 5, 8, 13?

TRIVIA QUIZ 48

1 MISCELLANY: What pseudonym did Eric Blair use?

2 GEOGRAPHY & TRAVEL: What is the next land mass you would come to travelling south from Sri Lanka?

3 PEOPLE: Which leader was nicknamed 'Il Duce'?

4 INVENTIONS: What psychological test did Hermann Rorschach devise?

5 HISTORY: In which war did the charge of the Light Brigade occur?

6 SPORT: Who did Arthur Ashe defeat in his memorable Wimbledon Men's Singles Final?

7 MUSIC: Who said it was 'extraordinary how potent cheap music is'?

8 SCIENCE: Who said 'I cannot believe that God plays dice with the cosmos'?

9 THE ARTS: Who responded to criticism about his lack of punctuation by including a page of commas and full-stops in a reprint of his book, inviting readers to put them where they wanted?

10 FILM, TV & RADIO: Who is the wife of cartoonist Gerald Scarfe?

11 NATURAL HISTORY: Which plant gives the most food per acre?

12 MISCELLANY: What material has the highest thermal conductivity?

▶ QUIZMASTER: Why is May 27 a significant date for horror movie stars Peter Cushing, Vincent Price and Christopher Lee?

ANSWERS 47

1 Obelix.

2 Brussels.

3 Henry Kissinger.

4 Cats' eyes

5 Boadicea or Boudicca.

6 Millwall.

7 Frankie Goes To Hollywood and Gerry And The Pacemakers.

8 Because it was discovered in 1789, not long after Uranus was first sighted.

9 Von Stalhein.

10 Loretta Lynn.

11 The Australian emu (it stands about five feet tall).

12 Juno, the others are various names of the goddess of beauty.

■ 21 (each number is the sum of the previous two).

ANSWERS 48

1 George Orwell.

2 Antarctica.

3 Benito Mussolini.

4 The Rorschach Test (or Ink Blot Test).

5 The Crimean War.

6 Jimmy Connors.

7 Noël Coward.

8 Albert Einstein.

9 Timothy Dexter.

10 Jane Asher.

11 The banana, which produces up to 20 tons.

12 Diamond.

■ It's their birthday.

TRIVIA QUIZ 49

1 MISCELLANY: Which one-eyed giants forged thunderbolts for Zeus?

2 GEOGRAPHY & TRAVEL: Which island was called The Island Of Saints in the Middle Ages?

3 PEOPLE: Where were Nazi war criminals tried after World War II?

4 INVENTIONS: What is the name of the device sometimes fitted to lorries to record speed and times of travel?

5 HISTORY: Who did the Earl of Bothwell marry in 1567?

6 SPORT: Which horse won the Derby, the St. Leger and the 2,000 Guineas in 1970?

7 MUSIC: Which pin-up upset girl fans at the Montreux Pop Festival by dying his hair black?

8 SCIENCE: What is the main use of L-Dopa?

9 THE ARTS: Who is George Smiley's Russian adversary in the spy stakes?

10 FILM, TV & RADIO: Which ventriloquist's dummy became the eponymous star of a radio show?

11 NATURAL HISTORY: What proboscis has 40,000 muscles?

12 MISCELLANY: A group of English writers came to be known as 'the angry young men' after the title of which play?

▶ **QUIZMASTER:** Who calls the tune?

TRIVIA QUIZ 50

1 MISCELLANY: What does the dog signify in medieval art?

2 GEOGRAPHY & TRAVEL: Which nation covers the largest area on the map?

3 PEOPLE: Who was Prime Minister of Britain when Edward VIII abdicated in 1936?

4 INVENTIONS: Where in the car would you put tetraethyl?

5 HISTORY: What nationality was Martin Luther?

6 SPORT: Which country was the first winner of soccer's World Cup?

7 MUSIC: Who wrote in his diary: 'Music and sweet women I cannot but give way to, whatever my business is.'?

8 SCIENCE: What did British physicist J.J. Thomson discover in 1897?

9 THE ARTS: In which novel does Manderley burn down?

10 FILM, TV & RADIO: In which educational establishment are Leroy and Doris taught by Mr Shorofsky and Lydia Grant?

11 NATURAL HISTORY: Which is the larger, the Asian or the African elephant?

12 MISCELLANY: Who was Jack Dawkins?

▶ **QUIZMASTER:** Why are children like old people when it comes to headaches?

ANSWERS 49

1 The Cyclops.

2 Ireland.

3 Nuremberg.

4 Tachograph.

5 Mary, Queen of Scots.

6 Nijinsky.

7 Simon Le Bon.

8 The treatment of Parkinson's disease.

9 Karla.

10 Archie (in *Educating Archie*, by Peter Brough).

11 The elephant's trunk.

12 John Osborne's *Look Back In Anger*.

■ He who pays the piper.

ANSWERS 50

1 Fidelity.

2 The Soviet Union.

3 Stanley Baldwin.

4 In the petrol tank (it's an anti-knock agent).

5 German.

6 Uruguay.

7 Samuel Pepys.

8 The electron.

9 *Rebecca* (by Daphne Du Maurier).

10 The High School For The Performing Arts (in *Fame*).

11 The African elephant.

12 The Artful Dodger.

■ They very rarely have them.

TRIVIA QUIZ 51

1 MISCELLANY: How did Anna Karenina die?

2 GEOGRAPHY & TRAVEL: Which semi-circular Greek island is the crater tip of a volcano?

3 PEOPLE: Who killed President Kennedy's assassin Lee Harvey Oswald?

4 INVENTIONS: What is the world's largest computer manufacturer?

5 HISTORY: Which island was awarded the George Cross for gallantry?

6 SPORT: In which field event can you use the flop or the scissors?

7 MUSIC: Which group had a hit with 'Down Under'?

8 SCIENCE: What was a Leyden jar used for?

9 THE ARTS: Which German author produced the best-seller *Mein Kampf*?

10 FILM, TV & RADIO: Who made the phrase 'Silly old moo' famous?

11 NATURAL HISTORY: What is a female fox called?

12 MISCELLANY: What is pâte feuilletée?

▶ QUIZMASTER: According to Greek mythology Prometheus created mankind out of which material?

TRIVIA QUIZ 52

1 MISCELLANY: Name either the 'heaven' or the 'hell' of Greek mythology.

2 GEOGRAPHY & TRAVEL: A bridge built by Abraham Darby in 1780 is the world's first cast iron civil engineering construction. Where is it?

3 PEOPLE: What sort of people wear yashmaks?

4 INVENTIONS: Which direction does a retro-rocket point?

5 HISTORY: Who was the victor at the Battle of Bannockburn?

6 SPORT: Who was the second Englishman to run the four-minute mile?

7 MUSIC: What is the usual material for the strings of a classical guitar?

8 SCIENCE: What physical element was discovered in the parish of Strontian, Argyllshire?

9 THE ARTS: Which sport is referred to in the title *Catcher In The Rye*?

10 FILM, TV & RADIO: An undertaking that she would not take her daughters to a political meeting until they were 12, was a condition of which actress's divorce?

11 NATURAL HISTORY: What is the name of a badger's home?

12 MISCELLANY: Which building did Sir Hugh Casson design for two-ton residents?

▶ QUIZMASTER: What is a runcible spoon?

ANSWERS 51

1 She threw herself under a train.

2 Santorini.

3 Jack Ruby.

4 IBM.

5 Malta.

6 The high jump.

7 Men At Work.

8 To store electricity.

9 Adolf Hitler.

10 Warren Mitchell (playing Alf Garnett in '*Till Death Us Do Part*').

11 A vixen.

12 Puff pastry.

■ Mud.

ANSWERS 52

1 Elysian Fields (heaven) and Tartarus (hell).

2 Ironbridge, Shropshire.

3 Moslem women.

4 Forwards.

5 Robert Bruce.

6 Derek Ibbotson.

7 Nylon.

8 Strontium.

9 Baseball

10 Vanessa Redgrave's.

11 A set.

12 The Elephant and Rhino House at London Zoo.

■ A fork used for pickles, curved like a spoon, with one sharp edge.

TRIVIA QUIZ 53

1 MISCELLANY: Who was the Roman god of love?

2 GEOGRAPHY & TRAVEL: What is the capital of Australia?

3 PEOPLE: Where did Queen Salote reign between 1918 and 1965?

4 INVENTIONS: How many tons of TNT does a megaton represent?

5 HISTORY: What was the most important book first published in the reign of James I?

6 SPORT: Who was World Snooker Champion before Steve Davis?

7 MUSIC: Who said: 'How charmingly sweet you sing'?

8 SCIENCE: What was the best weather news ten thousand years ago?

9 THE ARTS: What was Miss Joan Hunter-Dunn playing in John Betjeman's poem?

10 FILM, TV & RADIO: Tom and Barbara tried self-sufficiency in Suburbia. What was their surname?

11 NATURAL HISTORY: How do the butterwort and sundew plants vary their diet?

12 MISCELLANY: Which is the odd one out: Don Carlos, Don Giovanni, Don Juan?

▶ QUIZMASTER: What colour are Rupert Bear's trousers?

TRIVIA QUIZ 54

1 MISCELLANY: Which wine is flavoured with pine resin?

2 GEOGRAPHY & TRAVEL: What country has the highest exports on a per capita basis?

3 PEOPLE: What is the coming-of-age ceremony for Jewish boys?

4 INVENTIONS: What did the Swallow Sidecar Company change its name to in 1945?

5 HISTORY: Which English city holds a Goose Fair every year?

6 SPORT: Who did Muhammed Ali defeat to win the World Heavyweight Championship for the first time?

7 MUSIC: How many times has Dolly Parton been married?

8 SCIENCE: In what year did man first step on to the surface of the moon?

9 THE ARTS: Who defined his art as 'a talent to amuse'?

10 FILM, TV & RADIO: The film *Il Buono, Il Brutto, Il Cattivo* is better known to English speakers by what name?

11 NATURAL HISTORY: What is the regulation position for the wings of a butterfly, as opposed to those of a moth?

12 MISCELLANY: Who named his autobiography *Unreliable Memoirs*?

▶ QUIZMASTER: What is a philogynist?

ANSWERS 53

1 Cupid.

2 Canberra.

3 Tonga.

4 One million.

5 The authorised version of the *Bible*.

6 Terry Griffiths.

7 The Pussy Cat (in *The Owl And The Pussy Cat*).

8 The Ice Age had ended.

9 Tennis.

10 Good (in The Good Life).

11 They catch insects.

12 Don Carlos, the other two are names for the legendary profligate.

■ Yellow with a black grid pattern.

ANSWERS 54

1 Retsina.

2 Belgium.

3 Bar Mitzvah.

4 Jaguar Cars.

5 Nottingham.

6 Sonny Liston.

7 Once (to Carl Dean, the asphalt contractor she met in the Wishy Washy Laundromat on the first day she came to Nashville in 1964).

8 1969

9 Noël Coward.

10 The spaghetti western, *The Good, The Bad And The Ugly*.

11 A resting butterfly keeps its wings upright, the moth folds them level with its body.

12 Clive James.

■ An admirer of women.

TRIVIA QUIZ 55

1 MISCELLANY: What does NATO stand for?

2 GEOGRAPHY & TRAVEL: Which British poet is especially revered as a hero in Greece?

3 PEOPLE: Which writer invented one-upmanship?

4 INVENTIONS: What word in radio communication, means 'your message has been received and understood'?

5 HISTORY: Which English judge presided at the 'Bloody Assize'?

6 SPORT: What game involves flicking plastic discs into a container by pressing them sharply with other discs?

7 MUSIC: On which train through Carolina would you expect to be served ham and eggs?

8 SCIENCE: What is the laboratory name for oil of vitriol?

9 THE ARTS: Who was the heroine of a children's story featuring seven diminutive miners?

10 FILM, TV & RADIO: In which series would you expect to find Compo, Clegg and Foggy?

11 NATURAL HISTORY: What is a squirrel's home called?

12 MISCELLANY: Which Japanese alcoholic drink is brewed like beer?

▶ QUIZMASTER: What physical characteristic identifies a melanocomous person?

TRIVIA QUIZ 56

1 MISCELLANY: Which town is the setting for the last scene in *Tess Of The d'Urbervilles*?

2 GEOGRAPHY & TRAVEL: Who wrote *Journal Of A Landscape Painter In Greece And Albania*?

3 PEOPLE: Which member of the present royal family was born at Glamis Castle?

4 INVENTIONS: What is a microdot?

5 HISTORY: What title was given to the eldest sons of the kings of France before the revolution?

6 SPORT: How many foot faults can the server have in tennis before losing the point?

7 MUSIC: How many keys are there in a normal piano?

8 SCIENCE: What single unit is 5,880,000 million miles?

9 THE ARTS: Where was the Ancient Mariner's listener on his way to before he was buttonholed?

10 FILM, TV & RADIO: Who portrays Joan Crawford as an unloving mother in *Mommie Dearest*?

11 NATURAL HISTORY: What main feature differentiates the male house sparrow from the female?

12 MISCELLANY: In which part of the British Empire are local telephone calls free of charge?

▶ QUIZMASTER: Who said covetously: 'Poop poop, poop poop?

ANSWERS 55

1 North Atlantic Treaty Organisation.

2 Lord Byron.

3 Stephen Potter.

4 Roger.

5 Judge Jeffreys.

6 Tiddlywinks.

7 The Chattanooga Choo-Choo.

8 Sulphuric acid.

9 Snow White.

10 *The Last Of The Summer Wine.*

11 A drey.

12 Sake.

■ Black hair.

ANSWERS 56

1 Winchester, or 'Wintoncester'. (A black flag on a tower indicates that Tess has been executed.)

2 Edward Lear.

3 Princess Margaret.

4 A photograph reduced to the size of a dot.

5 Dauphin.

6 Two.

7 88.

8 One light year.

9 A wedding.

10 Faye Dunaway.

11 The male has a black bib.

12 Hong Kong

■ Mr. Toad (in *The Wind In The Willows*).

TRIVIA QUIZ 57 ▶

1 MISCELLANY: At what distance should you be able to read a number plate to satisfy the Ministry of Transport driving licence requirement.

2 GEOGRAPHY & TRAVEL: Which British city has the largest Chinese population?

3 PEOPLE: Name one of the first two men to walk on the moon.

4 INVENTIONS: What planet in our own solar system was only discovered in 1930?

5 HISTORY: What did the Toleration Act of 1689 do?

6 SPORT & LEISURE: In which sport is the Jules Rimet trophy contested?

7 MUSIC: Which Rolling Stones LP first appeared with a 3D picture on the cover of the group dressed as fantastic wizards?

8 SCIENCE: What can be 'up', 'down', are sometimes 'strange' and sometimes 'charmed'?

9 THE ARTS: Who invented Peter Rabbit?

10 FILM, TV & RADIO: Who is the wife of Desmond Wilcox?

11 NATURAL HISTORY: What is the catalogue name of the snapdragon?

12 MISCELLANY: Who or what are freebooters.

▶ **QUIZMASTER:** Who was the last prisoner to be held in the Tower of London?

TRIVIA QUIZ 58 ▶

1 MISCELLANY: How many people to the nearest 50 work inside the National Westminster Tower, London?

2 GEOGRAPHY & TRAVEL: Which nation grows the most mustard?

3 PEOPLE: What is the Society Of Friends more usually called?

4 INVENTIONS: What hooded jacket invented by the Eskimos have we adopted?

5 HISTORY: For what purpose was the Dome at Brighton originally built?

6 SPORT: What, in a Victorian meal, was the remove?

7 MUSIC: What is a ballerino?

8 SCIENCE: What is the scientific name for quicksilver?

9 THE ARTS: In which book was Shangri La found?

10 FILM, TV & RADIO: Which police series was built around a film called *The Blue Lamp*, despite the fact that its hero died at the end?

11 NATURAL HISTORY: Which animals breed to produce a mule?

12 MISCELLANY: What is the pseudonym of author David Cornwell?

▶ **QUIZMASTER:** Which woman has appeared on the cover of *Time* Magazine more times than any other?

ANSWERS 57

1 25 yards.

2 Manchester.

3 Neil Armstrong or Edwin Aldrin.

4 Pluto.

5 It established freedom of worship.

6 Football. (It's the correct name for the World Cup.)

7 *Their Satanic Majesties Request.*

8 Quarks (atomic particles).

9 Beatrix Potter.

10 Esther Rantzen.

11 Antirrhinum.

12 Pirates or bandits.

■ Rudolph Hess.

ANSWERS 58

1 2,500

2 Canada.

3 The Quakers.

4 The parka.

5 As a royal stables.

6 The main course.

7 A male ballet dancer.

8 Mercury.

9 *Lost Horizons* (by James Hilton).

10 *Dixon of Dock Green.*

11 A male donkey and a female horse.

12 John le Carré.

■ The Virgin Mary.

TRIVIA QUIZ 59

1 MISCELLANY: What does halcyon mean?

2 GEOGRAPHY & TRAVEL: Where is the annual Henley-on-Todd Regatta held?

3 PEOPLE: What position did U Thant hold between 1962 and 1972?

4 INVENTIONS: What is the 400,000 ton Ninian Central Platform?

5 HISTORY: Where was Davy Crockett killed?

6 SPORT: Which sportsmen contest the Ryder Cup?

7 MUSIC: The highest position any recording of Johnny B Goode reached in the British charts was 35. Who was the singer?

8 SCIENCE: Which way do tornadoes and cyclones tend to spin in the northern half of the globe?

9 THE ARTS: In which West End play is there a policeman called Trotter?

10 FILM, TV & RADIO: What was the name of the comic family featured in Frank Muir and Dennis Norden's *Take It From Here*?

11 NATURAL HISTORY: How does the earwig get its name?

12 MISCELLANY: How many words, to the nearest 100, are there in the average person's vocabulary?

▶ QUIZMASTER: Why should John Farynor have been more careful?

TRIVIA QUIZ 60

1 MISCELLANY: What percentage of British engineers, to the nearest five, are women?

2 GEOGRAPHY & TRAVEL: In which country did Gulliver discover a race of giants?

3 PEOPLE: Who was the first woman to take her place in the House Of Commons?

4 INVENTIONS: What amber globe was named after the 1931-37 Minister of Transport?

5 HISTORY: Which German was nicknamed The Iron Chancellor?

6 SPORT: What is the sporting significance of Putney and Mortlake?

7 MUSIC: What is the tempo of a piece of music?

8 SCIENCE: Who discovered radium in 1898?

9 THE ARTS: What is the trade of Bottom, the character in the ass's head in *A Midsummer Night's Dream*?

10 FILM, TV & RADIO: Who played the headmaster in the film of *The Browning Version*?

11 NATURAL HISTORY: What food would a gorilla choose if he was sent with a £5 note to the butcher?

12 MISCELLANY: What bird used to appear in chemists' shop signs?

▶ QUIZMASTER: Which Brixton street, celebrated in a hit song by Eddie Grant, was opened in the Victorian era, with 'novel' electric lighting for late night shopping?

ANSWERS 59

1 Calm.

2 Alice Springs, Australia. (The regatta is held in the dried-up river bed of the Todd. Holes are cut in the bottoms of boats so that competitors can run.

3 Secretary-General of the United Nations.

4 A North Sea oil well.

5 The Alamo.

6 Golfers.

7 Jimi Hendrix.

8 Anti-clockwise.

9 *The Mousetrap.*

10 The Glums.

11 Its wings are slightly ear-shaped.

12 8,000.

■ He was the baker who started the Great Fire Of London in 1666 by failing to damp down his oven.

ANSWERS 60

1 Two and a half per cent.

2 Brobdingnag.

3 Lady Astor.

4 The Belisha beacon.

5 Bismarck.

6 They are the starting and finishing points of the Oxford and Cambridge Boat Race.

7 The speed with which it is played.

8 Marie Curie.

9 A weaver.

10 Wilfred Hyde-White.

11 Nothing (gorillas are strictly vegetarian).

12 The phoenix.

■ Electric Avenue.

TRIVIA QUIZ 61

1 MISCELLANY: Which architect designed Centre Point?

2 GEOGRAPHY & TRAVEL: Where did Captain Cook die?

3 PEOPLE: What army rank is the equivalent of an admiral in the Royal Navy?

4 INVENTIONS: What is the identifying feature of a monkey-wrench?

5 HISTORY: Who was the only British king crowned on the field of battle?

6 SPORT: Where was the FA Cup held immediately before it moved to Wembley in 1923?

7 MUSIC: Which 50's singer is known as The Killer?

8 SCIENCE: Which Swiss eighteenth century mathematician published 886 books and memoirs?

9 THE ARTS: To which famous children's classic was *Good Wives* the sequel?

10 FILM, TV & RADIO: Who were the enemies of The Jets?

11 NATURAL HISTORY: What unsociable characteristic do the Gila Monster and the Mexican Beaded Lizard have in common?

12 MISCELLANY: Which ship sent the first SOS?

▶ QUIZMASTER: The largest eye of any creature ever found was 40cm long. What species did it belong to?

TRIVIA QUIZ 62

1 MISCELLANY: What year was the marriage between Prince Charles and Princess Diana?

2 GEOGRAPHY & TRAVEL: What is the world's largest island?

3 PEOPLE: By what popular term were the founders of the Social Democratic Party known?

4 INVENTIONS: What is the name given to concrete that arrives on the construction site in ready-made blocks?

5 HISTORY: When did British shoppers start using decimal currency?

6 SPORT: What event took place at Herne Hill, London during the 1948 Olympics?

7 MUSIC: What are the following: Electric Mistress, Cry Baby, Wah-Wah, Fuzz and Instant Funk?

8 SCIENCE: Why was 1939 a black year for insects?

9 THE ARTS: Who wrote *The Little Mermaid*?

10 FILM, TV & RADIO: Where would you find Little Joe and Hoss?

11 NATURAL HISTORY: What is a gasteropod with a spiral shell commonly called?

12 MISCELLANY: What was unusual about the narrator archy in Don Marquis' *archy and mehitabel*?

▶ QUIZMASTER: Who created the mini skirt?

ANSWERS 61

1 Colonel Richard Seifert.

2 Hawaii.

3 General.

4 A moveable jaw.

5 Henry VII.

6 Stamford Bridge.

7 Jerry Lee Lewis.

8 Leonard Euler.

9 *Little Women*.

10 The Sharks (in *West Side Story*).

11 They are both poisonous.

12 *The Titanic* in 1912 (before that the distress message was CQD).

■ A squid, itself 21 metres long - a heavyweight calamari.

ANSWERS 62

1 1981.

2 Greenland.

3 The Gang Of Four.

4 Pre-cast concrete.

5 1971.

6 Cycling.

7 They are all effects pedals which change the tone of an electric guitar.

8 DDT was developed.

9 Hans Christian Andersen.

10 *Bonanza*.

11 A snail.

12 He was a cockroach.

■ Mary Quant.

TRIVIA QUIZ 63

1 MISCELLANY: What are listed in the Stanley Gibbons Catalogue?

2 GEOGRAPHY & TRAVEL: What was the original function of Dr George Merryweather's Tempest Prognosticator, a machine activated by the movement of leeches, now at Whitby Museum?

3 PEOPLE: Which saint would you call on if you lost something?

4 INVENTIONS: What is the name of a road crossing with traffic lights operated by pedestrians?

5 HISTORY: Antigone Costanda achieved fame in 1951 with her 40-26-38 inch figure. How?

6 SPORT: Which Charlton Athletic half-back played for Scotland without ever having been there?

7 MUSIC: What was Mozart's favourite instrument?

8 SCIENCE: What was discovered by the chance contamination of a dish at St Mary's Hospital, Paddington, London in 1928?

9 THE ARTS: Name either the play or the film made from the novel *Mr Norris Changes Trains*.

10 FILM, TV & RADIO: Which actor took over Paul Scofield's role in *The Shooting Party* when he broke his leg?

11 NATURAL HISTORY: What are the so-called 'Barbary apes' on the island of Gibraltar

12 MISCELLANY: Which Wild West train robber is thought to have escaped his pursuers and adopted a new life in New York running a weighing machine business?

▶ **QUIZMASTER:** How many people can hear an apthong?

TRIVIA QUIZ 64

1 MISCELLANY: Which former MP unsuccessfully staged his own suicide in 1973?

2 GEOGRAPHY & TRAVEL: Which is the only London underground station with a platform bar?

3 PEOPLE: What is another name for a chief priest?

4 INVENTIONS: What is the symbol for hydrogen?

5 HISTORY: Which of Henry VIII's wives outlived him?

6 SPORT: In football, which is the only English or Scottish league team with a 'J' in the name?

7 MUSIC: What took place on a New York State dairy farm belonging to Max Yasgur in 1969?

8 SCIENCE: If the entire history of the Earth was represented by a single year, in which month would the first mammals appear?

9 THE ARTS: Which former Etonian author served once as a policeman in Burma?

10 FILM, TV & RADIO: Who is the third party of a Truffaut triangle made up by Catherine and Jules?

11 NATURAL HISTORY: What animal's hair is traditionally used to make shaving brushes?

12 MISCELLANY: Which policeman gave up his job to become a professional snooker player?

▶ **QUIZMASTER:** Why did two and a half million gloomy Dutchmen have to walk home in 1982?

ANSWERS 63

1 Postage stamps.

2 It was supposed to forecast storms.

3 Saint Antony of Padua.

4 A pelican crossing.

5 She was the first Miss World.

6 John Hewie (he was South African but his father was Scottish).

7 The viola.

8 Penicillin.

9 The play was *I Am A Camera* and the film was *Cabaret*.

10 James Mason.

11 Macaque monkeys.

12 Butch Cassidy.

■ None. It's a silent letter, like 'g' in gnat.

ANSWERS 64

1 John Stonehouse.

2 Sloane Square.

3 A Pontiff.

4 H.

5 Catherine Parr.

6 St Johnstone.

7 Woodstock Festival.

8 December.

9 George Orwell.

10 Jim.

11 Badger's.

12 Ray Reardon.

■ Their bicycles had been stolen.

TRIVIA QUIZ 65

1 MISCELLANY: What do the letters IMF stand for?

2 GEOGRAPHY & TRAVEL: Why does London's Isle Of Dogs have place-names like Cuba Street, Havannah Street and Tobago Street?

3 PEOPLE: Who reached the summit of Everest with Hillary in 1953?

4 INVENTIONS: What reduction is indicated when a measurement is prefixed by 'pico'?

5 HISTORY: What disaster hit Ireland between 1845 and 1849?

6 SPORT: How many players are there in a basketball team?

7 MUSIC: Who are Yum-Yum and Nanki-Poo?

8 SCIENCE: What fell on Cumbria to a depth of 257 inches in 1954?

9 THE ARTS: Who is Jeeves' young master?

10 FILM, TV & RADIO: What was Much Binding In The Marsh, before it became a country club and then a radio show?

11 NATURAL HISTORY: Where on a horse are the withers?

12 MISCELLANY: Why was tile-making a dangerous job in the 19th century?

QUIZMASTER: Who was Frankenstein?

TRIVIA QUIZ 66

1 MISCELLANY: Why do salmon swim hundreds of miles upstream, risking waterfalls and anglers?

2 GEOGRAPHY & TRAVEL: Why is Qantas spelt without a u after the q?

3 PEOPLE: Who bought *The Times* in 1981?

4 INVENTIONS: What is the name of a mass-produced electric circuit with conductive strips not wires?

5 HISTORY: In which wars did Yorkists fight Lancastrians?

6 SPORT: Which cricketer captained England and also won honours in fencing?

7 MUSIC: What do The Specials, The Fun Boy Three and The Colour Field have in common?

8 SCIENCE: Name two of the three planets with rings.

9 THE ARTS: Which Shakespearean play inspired an interpretation with music by Bernstein, lyrics by Sondheim and a character called Officer Krupke?

10 FILM, TV & RADIO: Which TV series resulted from the stories a former Liverpool teacher used to tell his pupils?

11 NATURAL HISTORY: What is amber?

12 MISCELLANY: When were the first Olympic Games staged: 1010 BC, 776 BC, 1081 or 1282?

QUIZMASTER: Who is the most famous inhabitant of Yellowstone Park?

ANSWERS 65

1 International Monetary Fund.

2 Because of its proximity to West India Docks.

3 Sherpa Tensing.

4 A million, millionth part.

5 The terrible potato famine.

6 Five.

7 The two lovers in *The Mikado*.

8 Rain (it's Britain's highest recorded rainfall).

9 Bertie Wooster.

10 An RAF station.

11 The highest part of the back, between the shoulder blades.

12 The lead in the glaze caused premature deaths.

■ A student who created a monster out of parts of other corpses in Mary Shelley's gothic novel.

ANSWERS 66

1 To mate and give birth.

2 Because it's an acronym (for Queensland And Northern Territories Air Service).

3 Rupert Murdoch.

4 A printed circuit.

5 The Wars Of The Roses.

6 Rachel Hayhoe-Flint.

7 Terry Hall.

8 Jupiter, Saturn or Uranus.

9 *Romeo And Juliet*, as the musical, *West Side Story*.

10 *Scully* (by Alan Bleasdale).

11 Fossilized pine or fir resin.

12 776 BC.

■ Yogi Bear.

TRIVIA QUIZ 67

1 MISCELLANY: Which book, by Harriet Beecher Stowe was subtitled *Life Among The Lowly*?

2 GEOGRAPHY & TRAVEL: Where on the North Yorkshire moors is the landscape dominated by three giant spheres?

3 PEOPLE: Who rides in procession to the London Courts of Justice every November?

4 INVENTIONS: Which company patented the pneumatic tyre?

5 HISTORY: What famous mutiny took place in 1857?

6 SPORT: What was unusual about the 721 runs scored by the Australian cricket team against England one day in 1948?

7 MUSIC: Which popular American tune was borrowed as a theme in the finale of Dvořák's *New World Symphony*?

8 SCIENCE: What did Einstein publish in 1905?

9 THE ARTS: Who drew the Mr Men?

10 FILM, TV & RADIO: Who does David Soul play in *Starsky And Hutch*?

11 NATURAL HISTORY: Match these three animals with their environments: tortoise/terrapin/turtle; freshwater/sea/land.

12 MISCELLANY: Who designed the Houses of Parliament, but died before they were completed?

▶ QUIZMASTER: Who, when talking about poor countries, said: 'The US has much to offer the Third World War'?

TRIVIA QUIZ 68

1 MISCELLANY: Who founded the Pre-Raphaelite Brotherhood in 1848?

2 GEOGRAPHY & TRAVEL: Who discovered the continent of America and never realised it?

3 PEOPLE: What are the names of Princess Anne's two children?

4 INVENTIONS: What form of transport did Sir Christopher Cockerell invent?

5 HISTORY: Whose assassination precipitated World War I?

6 SPORT: In which card game is the expression 'one for his nob' used?

7 MUSIC: What was Sid Vicious' real name?

8 SCIENCE: How many moons, to the nearest 10, would equal the weight of the earth?

9 THE ARTS: Which detective had an assistant called Tinker?

10 FILM, TV & RADIO: *The Magnificent Seven* is a version of what 1954 film?

11 NATURAL HISTORY: How far can a mole dig in an hour?

12 MISCELLANY: Where would you find these items: couter, pauldron, vambrace and cuisse?

▶ QUIZMASTER: What is the world's most common first name?

ANSWERS 67

1 *Uncle Tom's Cabin*.

2 Fylingdales (site of an impressive early warning listening station).

3 The Lord Mayor.

4 Michelin.

5 The Indian Mutiny.

6 It was the highest number of runs ever scored in a day in England.

7 Yankee Doodle.

8 His special theory of relativity.

9 Roger Hargreaves.

10 Hutch.

11 Tortoise/land; terrapin/freshwater; turtle/sea.

12 Sir Charles Barry.

■ Ronald Reagan.

ANSWERS 68

1 Dante Gabriel Rossetti.

2 Christopher Columbus (who thought he was off the eastern coast of Asia).

3 Peter and Zara.

4 The hovercraft.

5 Archduke Franz Ferdinand of Austria.

6 Cribbage.

7 John Simon Ritchie.

8 81.

9 Sexton Blake.

10 Kurosawa's *Seven Samurai*.

11 15 feet.

12 In suits of armour.

■ Mohammed.

TRIVIA QUIZ 69

1 MISCELLANY: What is the Sheffield silver hallmark, which has been in use since 1773?

2 GEOGRAPHY & TRAVEL: In which cities are the Parthenon and the Pantheon?

3 PEOPLE: Who was the leader of the Solidarity movement in Poland?

4 INVENTIONS: Why did Pat Simmons stop talking on April 2, 1985?

5 HISTORY: What was Wells Fargo's main form of transport?

6 SPORT: Which rowing club stages the Henley Regatta?

7 MUSIC: Which opera is 20 hours long and had a special theatre built for its first performance?

8 SCIENCE: What did Röntgen discover to win the first Nobel Prize For Physics in 1901?

9 THE ARTS: What was Superman's alias?

10 FILM, TV & RADIO: Who was born Marion Michael Morrison?

11 NATURAL HISTORY: Which member of the camel family has no hump?

12 MISCELLANY: Which war hero gave his name to a type of footwear?

▶ QUIZMASTER: What kind of mosquito is vegetarian?

TRIVIA QUIZ 70

1 MISCELLANY: What is Shakespeare's shortest play?

2 GEOGRAPHY & TRAVEL: At 12 noon on Christmas day in London, what time is it in Paris?

3 PEOPLE: Who built the Menai Suspension Bridge?

4 INVENTIONS: What is the shorter term for light amplification by the simulated emission of radiation?

5 HISTORY: Which king was nicknamed 'Coeur de Lion'?

6 SPORT: In which game must the skittles not be knocked down?

7 MUSIC: What is the name of BB King's guitar?

8 SCIENCE: What returns to the night sky every 76 years?

9 THE ARTS: Which American playwright wrote *A Streetcar Named Desire*?

10 FILM, TV & RADIO: What, in retrospect, makes the 1951 film *Bedtime For Bonzo* irresistably fascinating?

11 NATURAL HISTORY: Why is the Scottish crossbill a particularly patriotic bird?

12 MISCELLANY: Who wrote under the pen-name of George Eliot?

▶ QUIZMASTER: What form did the three heads of Hecate take?

ANSWERS 69

1 A crown.

2 The Parthenon is in Athens, the Pantheon in Rome.

3 Lech Walesa.

4 Her talking clock recording was replaced by a man's voice.

5 The stagecoach.

6 Leander.

7 Wagner's *Der Ring Des Nibelungen* (The Nibelung's Ring).

8 X-rays.

9 Clark Kent.

10 John Wayne.

11 The Llama.

12 The Duke of Wellington.

■ The male mosquito.

ANSWERS 70

1 *Macbeth.*

2 12 noon.

3 Thomas Telford.

4 Laser.

5 Richard I.

6 Bar billiards.

7 Lucille.

8 Halley's Comet.

9 Tennessee Williams.

10 Ronald Reagan appeared in it with an ape.

11 It is only found in Britain.

12 Marian Evans.

■ A horse, a dog and a lion.

TRIVIA QUIZ 71

1 MISCELLANY: What was the poet Percy Shelley's middle name?

2 GEOGRAPHY & TRAVEL: What country to Chinese Buddhists is the Holy Land?

3 PEOPLE: Who is the Saudi Arabian oil minister?

4 INVENTIONS: What is the name of an unmanned spacecraft on an exploratory mission?

5 HISTORY: How many of the 12 apostles died a natural death?

6 SPORT: What would you be doing if you were pollarding?

7 MUSIC: What lively Neapolitan dance was named after a spider?

8 SCIENCE: What travels toward the earth at between 100 and 1,000 mph and returns at 87,000 mph (nearly half the speed of light)?

9 THE ARTS: Which book features the love affair of Connie and Mellors?

10 FILM, TV & RADIO: Who played Mr Peters in *Worzel Gummidge*?

11 NATURAL HISTORY: The sound of which insect was once thought to be an omen of imminent death?

12 MISCELLANY: Who was sent to kill the nine-headed monster Hydra?

▶ QUIZMASTER: What was the obsessive philosophy of the Small-endians in *Gulliver's Travels*?

TRIVIA QUIZ 72

1 MISCELLANY: What colour is Reisling wine?

2 GEOGRAPHY & TRAVEL: From what does Moscow take its name?

3 PEOPLE: By what name is Lesley Hornby better known?

4 INVENTIONS: What word did nuclear physics borrow from James Joyce's *Finnegan's Wake*?

5 HISTORY: How old was Mary Stuart when she became Queen of Scotland?

6 SPORT: Who won the first single-handed round-the-world yacht race?

7 MUSIC: Who is the A in A & M?

8 SCIENCE: Which science deals with matter and energy?

9 THE ARTS: Which story had a fairy called Tinker Bell?

10 FILM, TV & RADIO: How long is Edgar Reitz's film history of a German village, *Heimat*?

11 NATURAL HISTORY: What is ambergris?

12 MISCELLANY: Which Christmas decoration is said to have been an important symbol at Druid human sacrifices?

▶ QUIZMASTER: Which Hindu god's name is now also used to describe heavy lorries?

ANSWERS 71

1 Bysshe.

2 India.

3 Sheikh Yamani.

4 A probe.

5 One (St John the Evangelist).

6 Pruning a tree.

7 The tarantella (named after the tarantula).

8 Lightning.

9 *Lady Chatterley's Lover*.

10 Mike Berry.

11 The death-watch beetle.

12 Hercules.

■ They believed boiled eggs should be opened at the small end.

ANSWERS 72

1 White.

2 From the river Moscowa on which it is built.

3 Twiggy.

4 Quark.

5 Six days.

6 Robin Knox-Johnston.

7 Herb Alpert.

8 Physics.

9 Peter Pan.

10 16 hours.

11 A wax-like material produced in the intestines of the sperm whale and found floating in the sea.

12 Mistletoe.

■ Juggernaut, because of the enormous wooden ceremonial machine that is dragged into his temple every year.

TRIVIA QUIZ 73

1 MISCELLANY: Where would you find a serif?

2 GEOGRAPHY & TRAVEL: What, to the nearest 10 million, is the population of China?

3 PEOPLE: The British international car registration mark is GB. What is the Swiss?

4 INVENTIONS: What is a quarter-light?

5 HISTORY: Which country refused to join the EEC in 1973?

6 SPORT: In which sport do toxopholoists compete?

7 MUSIC: Which partner of Mary Ford designed and gave his name to a famous guitar?

8 SCIENCE: What is the brightest star in the night sky?

9 THE ARTS: Who was the chief pig in *Animal Farm*?

10 FILM, TV & RADIO: Who priced himself out of the lead role of *Apocalypse Now* by demanding $3 million for three weeks' work?

11 NATURAL HISTORY: In what form does Hanuman, Indian god of magic and healing, manifest himself?

12 MISCELLANY: What is a Shazadah?

▶ **QUIZMASTER:** What is a snailery?

TRIVIA QUIZ 74

1 MISCELLANY: What is the word for descending a precipice by sliding down a doubled rope?

2 GEOGRAPHY & TRAVEL: What is the most westerly terminus of the Piccadilly line?

3 PEOPLE: Which famous fighter pilot of World War II lost both legs?

4 INVENTIONS: What close-fitting garment worn by dancers is named after a 19th century French trapeze artist?

5 HISTORY: When was the breath test introduced to the UK?

6 SPORT: In which card game do you 'meld'?

7 MUSIC: Why was Al Martino's 'Here In My Heart' in 1952 the fastest single to reach number one after entering the British charts?

8 SCIENCE: What is the limit reached at −273.15 degrees centigrade?

9 THE ARTS: Name six of the Seven Deadly Sins?

10 FILM, TV & RADIO: Whose autobiography is titled *Sparks Fly Upwards*?

11 NATURAL HISTORY: Why do flies rub their legs together?

12 MISCELLANY: What would you do with a julep?

▶ **QUIZMASTER:** What is the difference between a TV serial and a TV series?

ANSWERS 73

1 On a printed letter (it's a little decorative flourish at the top or bottom of the letter on some typefaces).

2 1,082 million.

3 CH.

4 A small side window in a car.

5 Norway.

6 Archery.

7 Les Paul.

8 Sirius.

9 Napoleon.

10 Steve McQueen.

11 In the form of a rhesus monkey.

12 A Shah's son.

■ A snail farm.

ANSWERS 74

1 Abseiling.

2 Heathrow.

3 Group Captain Douglas Bader.

4 The leotard.

5 1967.

6 Canasta.

7 Because it went into the first chart ever compiled.

8 It's the lowest possible centigrade temperature.

9 Lust, pride, anger, envy, sloth, avarice, gluttony.

10 Stewart Granger's.

11 To clean themselves by scraping off the dirt.

12 Drink it.

■ A serial is a single story divided into episodes; a series is a regular succession of self-contained stories with common themes or characters.

TRIVIA QUIZ 75

1 MISCELLANY: What happened at 3am on August 3, 1963 at Sears Crossing, Buckinghamshire?

2 GEOGRAPHY & TRAVEL: Why was Greenland so named?

3 PEOPLE: What kind of people are members of the NUS?

4 INVENTIONS: Who patented a waterproof material in 1835, consisting of cloth coated with india-rubber?

5 HISTORY: Which Englishwoman campaigned for improved prison conditions in the 19th century?

6 SPORT: Which boxer gave up halfway through a title fight with Sugar Ray Leonard?

7 MUSIC: Who was 'tall and tanned and young and lovely'?

8 SCIENCE: What takes Saturn almost 30 years to complete?

9 THE ARTS: Which artist's life is depicted in the film *Moulin Rouge*?

10 FILM, TV & RADIO: Which singer/comedian travelled to the USA to see how he could adapt his material to American Football?

11 NATURAL HISTORY: How many legs does a spider have?

12 GEOGRAPHY & TRAVEL: Which London shopping arcade is patrolled by Beadles?

▶ **QUIZMASTER:** In what month was Julius Caesar born?

TRIVIA QUIZ 76

1 MISCELLANY: Who said 'Let them eat cake!'?

2 GEOGRAPHY & TRAVEL: How many bridges cross the Tyne at Newcastle-upon-Tyne.

3 PEOPLE: What does a stevedore do?

4 INVENTIONS: Which city was linked to New York by Alexander Graham Bell's first cross-country telephone call?

5 HISTORY: Which monarch signed the Magna Carta at Runnymede?

6 SPORT: Which is the highest hand in poker, a run, a flush or a full house?

7 MUSIC: What is the name of the indigenous music of the French-speaking settlers of Louisiana?

8 SCIENCE: What gas glows red when electric current is passed through it?

9 THE ARTS: Name two of the four musketeers.

10 FILM, TV & RADIO: Name two of the three TV series in which Inspector Barlow appears?

11 NATURAL HISTORY: Who are more likely to be colour-blind, men or women?

12 MISCELLANY: What is marchpane?

▶ **QUIZMASTER:** What holidays were instigated by banker Sir John Lubbock?

ANSWERS 75

1 The Great Train Robbery.

2 To encourage settlers to go there.

3 Students (National Union of Students).

4 Charles Macintosh.

5 Elizabeth Fry.

6 Roberto Duran.

7 The girl from Ipanema.

8 A circuit of the Sun.

9 Toulouse-Lautrec's.

10 Max Boyce.

11 Eight.

12 Burlington Arcade.

■ July (the month was named after him).

ANSWERS 76

1 Marie Antoinette.

2 Five.

3 Loads and unloads ships.

4 Chicago.

5 King John.

6 A run.

7 Cajun.

8 Neon.

9 Athos, Porthos, Aramis and D'Artagnan.

10 *Z Cars, Softly Softly*, and *Barlow & Watt*.

11 Men.

12 Marzipan.

■ Bank holidays.

TRIVIA QUIZ 77

1 MISCELLANY: What is the most popular proprietary board game in the world?

2 GEOGRAPHY & TRAVEL: In which country is Timbuktu?

3 PEOPLE: Who was told by the Vienna Fine Arts Academy that his gift lay in architecture when he failed its entrance exam in 1908?

4 INVENTIONS: Where was the compass invented?

5 HISTORY: For which industry did Lavenham in Suffolk become famous?

6 SPORT: What colour is worn by the number five dog in greyhound racing?

7 MUSIC: Who wrote 'Psycho', a country song whose narrator kills four people and a puppy?

8 SCIENCE: What did Sir Humphrey Davy discover in 1801?

9 THE ARTS: What was the name of the Hunchback Of Notre Dame?

10 FILM, TV & RADIO: Which pop TV programme invited a panel of star guests to judge recent record releases 'hit' or 'miss'?

11 NATURAL HISTORY: How can you tell a weasel and a stoat apart by their tails?

12 MISCELLANY: Who invented the Rubik Cube?

▶ **QUIZMASTER:** What were the 'Bradburys' issued in 1914 by the British government?

TRIVIA QUIZ 78

1 MISCELLANY: How many sides are there in a dodecagon?

2 GEOGRAPHY & TRAVEL: Which European country is bordered on three sides by communist countries?

3 PEOPLE: By what other name is 'La Cosa Nostra' also known?

4 INVENTIONS: What was Stephenson's first locomotive called?

5 HISTORY: What is the name of the race of female warriors, said to have lived in Asia Minor?

6 SPORT: Where is the Welsh Grand National run?

7 MUSIC: How long would a bassoon be if it was stretched out?

8 SCIENCE: If the history of the earth is represented by a single year, when was Jesus born?

9 THE ARTS: Name the Christian names of two of the three literary Brontë sisters.

10 FILM, TV & RADIO: Who is the wife of Sam Shepard?

11 NATURAL HISTORY: How did the cuckoo flower get its name?

12 MISCELLANY: What are thribbles and censers?

▶ **QUIZMASTER:** What did the Norwegian Major Vidkun Quisling do to get his surname in the dictionary?

ANSWERS 77

1 Monopoly.

2 Mali

3 Adolf Hitler.

4 China.

5 Wool.

6 Orange

7 Leon Payne.

8 Magnesium.

9 Quasimodo.

10 *Juke Box Jury.*

11 The stoat has a black tip to its tail.

12 Professor Rubik.

■ The World War I pound note (hastily introduced to replace sovereigns, which were withdrawn because of their high gold content).

ANSWERS 78

1 12.

2 Austria.

3 The Mafia.

4 Locomotion

5 The Amazons

6 Chepstow.

7 Nine feet.

8 One second before midnight on December 31.

9 Charlotte, Emily and Anne.

10 Jessica Lange.

11 It was supposed to flower on the day the first cuckoo calls.

12 Vessels used to hold burning incense.

■ He collaborated with the Germans in 1940. (Quisling has come to mean collaborationist.)

TRIVIA QUIZ 79

1 MISCELLANY: What is Hansard?

2 GEOGRAPHY & TRAVEL: Which mountain range is climbed by the world's highest railway?

3 PEOPLE: What, in the Roman Catholic sense, is a Devil's advocate?

4 INVENTIONS: What mass-produced item cost $950 in 1909 and $290 in 1925?

5 HISTORY: Which is the oldest passenger railway station in London?

6 SPORT: Which sport is contested for the Swaythling Trophy?

7 MUSIC: Which composer wrote a work for instrumentalists and short-wave radios?

8 SCIENCE: What book, written by Isaac Newton, is regarded as the world's greatest single work of science?

9 THE ARTS: In which town was Tom Brown's school?

10 FILM, TV & RADIO: A new Merseyside estate is the setting for which soap opera?

11 NATURAL HISTORY: Bufo bufo is the scientific name for what creature?

12 MISCELLANY: What is the mythical creature with the head and arms of a man and the body and legs of a horse?

▶ **QUIZMASTER:** What is a group of kangaroos called?

TRIVIA QUIZ 80

1 MISCELLANY: Where would you expect a rabbit punch to land?

2 GEOGRAPHY & TRAVEL: Which is nearer to London, Leeds or Bradford?

3 PEOPLE: Which racing driver was killed while flying his own aircraft?

4 INVENTIONS: Why is the rhesus factor in blood so named?

5 HISTORY: Who lived at Bateman's, Burwash, Sussex?

6 SPORT: How many squares are there along one side of a Scrabble board?

7 MUSIC: What do 'Why Can't We Live Together?', 'Cherry Pie' and 'Your Love is King' have in common?

8 SCIENCE: Almost four fifths of the air is made up of what?

9 THE ARTS: Which writer produced the *Foundation Saga*?

10 FILM, TV & RADIO: Who played Sergeant Bilko?

11 NATURAL HISTORY: What are young hares called?

12 MISCELLANY: What is semiotics?

▶ **QUIZMASTER:** Which song about Christmas was a hit in mid-summer 1956?

ANSWERS 79

1 The official record of debates in the House of Commons.

2 The Andes.

3 The official who puts the case against the beatification or canonization of a candidate.

4 The Model T Ford.

5 London Bridge.

6 Table Tennis.

7 Karlheinz Stockhausen.

8 The *Principia Mathematica*.

9 Rugby.

10 *Brookside*.

11 The common toad.

12 A centaur.

■ A mob.

ANSWERS 80

1 On the neck.

2 Leeds.

3 Graham Hill.

4 Because it was first discovered in a rhesus monkey.

5 Rudyard Kipling.

6 15.

7 They are all tracks on Sade's album *Diamond Life*.

8 Nitrogen.

9 Isaac Asimov.

10 Phil Silvers.

11 Leverets.

12 The study of signs and symbols.

■ 'I'm Walking Backwards For Christmas', by The Goons.

TRIVIA QUIZ 81

1 MISCELLANY: Who draws the cartoon Fred Bassett?

2 GEOGRAPHY & TRAVEL: What happened at the Pollard Rock on March 18, 1967?

3 PEOPLE: Where would you find crofters?

4 INVENTIONS: What goes round and round in a police car's light?

5 HISTORY: Which husband and wife were the only British monarchs to rule jointly as king and queen?

6 SPORT: How many hoops are there on a full-size croquet court?

7 MUSIC: Which star comes from Luton but feels at home wherever his hat is?

8 SCIENCE: What was defined by law as precisely 4,840 square yards in 1305?

9 THE ARTS: Which humorist's middle name was Klapka?

10 FILM, TV & RADIO: What is the name of Radio Two's Sunday tea-time programme which features the Cliff Adams Singers?

11 NATURAL HISTORY: How much blood is contained in the average human body?

12 MISCELLANY: To what did fashionable people start giving the name settee after 1880?

▶ **QUIZMASTER:** Signor Bona Slang hung by his nose to arouse the desires of young girls. By what description is he better known?

TRIVIA QUIZ 82

▶

1 MISCELLANY: Which form of wrestling is won by forcing the opponent to touch the ground with any part of his body but his feet?

2 GEOGRAPHY & TRAVEL: What is Scotland's oil city?

3 PEOPLE: Which country has the largest army in the world?

4 INVENTIONS: What was accomplished for the first time in the Gossamer Albatross in 1979?

5 HISTORY: Where was the second atomic bomb dropped?

6 SPORT: Name one of the two substitutes who came on too late in England's last World Cup game of 1982.

7 MUSIC: Which Russian ballet dancer defected to the West in 1961?

8 SCIENCE: What is the name we use today for fluxioons, a mathematical concept developed by Sir Isaac Newton?

9 THE ARTS: With which three words does the Bible start?

10 FILM, TV & RADIO: What was a secretary referring to in 1927 when she said, 'It looks like my Uncle Oscar!'?

11 NATURAL HISTORY: What kind of creature is the Monarch, that often journeys from Canada to Mexico?

12 MISCELLANY: What is the English version of the American word broiling?

▶ **QUIZMASTER:** What is made of acrylonitrile butadiene styrene and covered with 100% pure blue wool?

ANSWERS 81

1 Graham.

2 The Torrey Canyon ran aground.

3 Scotland.

4 The reflector.

5 William III and Mary II.

6 Six.

7 Paul Young.

8 The acre.

9 Jerome K. Jerome.

10 *Sing Something Simple.*

11 9 pints.

12 The sofa.

■ 'The daring young man on the flying trapeze.'

ANSWERS 82

1 Sumo wrestling.

2 Aberdeen.

3 China.

4 A man-powered flight across the English Channel.

5 Nagasaki.

6 Kevin Keegan and Trevor Brooking.

7 Rudolph Nureyev.

8 Calculus.

9 'In the beginning'.

10 The first statuette for what has come to be known as the Oscar Awards.

11 A butterfly.

12 Grilling.

■ A policeman's helmet.

TRIVIA QUIZ 83

1 MISCELLANY: Which of these has least calories: a shot of gin, a glass of medium sherry, a 4oz glass of dry white wine?

2 GEOGRAPHY & TRAVEL: What would you use a gettoni token for in Italy?

3 PEOPLE: Who is the leader of the TUC?

4 INVENTIONS: Which of these materials can't be used as a container in a microwave oven: metal, glass, plastic?

5 HISTORY: What was held in the Crystal Palace in London in 1851?

6 SPORT: How many pawns does a chess player start with?

7 MUSIC: Which group did Stevie Winwood join at the age of 16?

8 SCIENCE: Who discovered in 1860 that carbolic acid is an antiseptic?

9 THE ARTS: Who was Dr Jekyll when he wasn't feeling himself?

10 FILM, TV & RADIO: Which much-loved character was 'killed off' in a fire on BBC radio to compete for an audience tuning in to the first ITV broadcast?

11 NATURAL HISTORY: How many toes does a cat have on its front paw?

12 MISCELLANY: What is the style of decoration that gives the illusion of three dimensional reality to painted surfaces?

▶ **QUIZMASTER:** What is the more respectful name for a 'trickcyclist'?

TRIVIA QUIZ 84

1 MISCELLANY: What is the hybrid of the grapefruit and tangerine?

2 GEOGRAPHY & TRAVEL: What is the maximum amount of duty-free whisky a person of 17 can bring into Britain?

3 PEOPLE: Which profession would you belong to if you had FRIBA after your name?

4 INVENTIONS: To which country was the murderer Crippin trying to escape when he was caught?

5 HISTORY: What was the French resistance movement called in World War II?

6 SPORT: What age are Derby runners?

7 MUSIC: How many players are there in the average symphony orchestra?

8 SCIENCE: What science was pioneered by the shivery-named Zygmunt Florenty von Wroblewsky?

9 THE ARTS: Which detective played the violin and took cocaine for relaxation?

10 FILM, TV & RADIO: What is the name of the M.A.S.H. theme song?

11 NATURAL HISTORY: What is a female red deer called?

12 MISCELLANY: What is the term for someone who eats no meat, fish or dairy products?

▶ **QUIZMASTER:** How was the original Jumbo killed in 1885?

ANSWERS 83

1 The sherry.

2 Making a call from an outside phone box.

3 Norman Willis.

4 Metal.

5 The Great Exhibition.

6 Eight.

7 The Spencer Davis Group.

8 Dr Lister.

9 Mr Hyde.

10 Grace Archer.

11 Five.

12 Trompe l'oeil.

■ A psychiatrist.

ANSWERS 84

1 The ugli.

2 One litre.

3 Architecture (Fellow of the Royal Institute of British Architects).

4 Canada.

5 The Maquis.

6 Three.

7 90.

8 Cryogenics – the study of low temperatures.

9 Sherlock Holmes.

10 'Suicide Is Painless'.

11 A hind.

12 A vegan.

■ A train collided with him (he was a circus elephant).

TRIVIA QUIZ 85 ▶

1 MISCELLANY: What is the main reason washing machines are fitted with a reverse tumble action?

2 GEOGRAPHY & TRAVEL: Where is the Meteorological Office?

3 PEOPLE: Where was Sir Winston Churchill's country home?

4 INVENTIONS: Where would you find a woofer and tweeter?

5 HISTORY: Where was Thomas à Becket murdered?

6 SPORT & LEISURE: What in sport was known as 'Henry's Hammer'?

7 MUSIC: Who wrote The Monkees hit 'I'm A Believer'?

8 SCIENCE: There is estimated to be just half a gram of astatine in the Earth's crust. What unique distinction does that give it?

9 THE ARTS: What was the real name of 'The Saint' in Leslie Charteris' books?

10 FILM, TV & RADIO: What recent film was advertised with the catchline 'Dead in the heart of Texas'?

11 NATURAL HISTORY: What creature can jump 200 times its own body length?

12 MISCELLANY: What popular dance did the New York musical *Runnin' Wild* introduce in 1923?

▶ **QUIZMASTER:** What are painted ladies, speckled woods and wall browns?

TRIVIA QUIZ 86 ▶

1 MISCELLANY: What happens to a surfer who wipes-out?

2 GEOGRAPHY & TRAVEL: In which ocean are the Turks and Caicos Islands?

3 PEOPLE: Who founded the National Viewers' and Listeners' Association?

4 INVENTIONS: What is a duplex radiant ring on an electric cooker?

5 HISTORY: When did the half crown cease to be legal tender?

6 SPORT: Which country won the soccer World Cup in 1982?

7 MUSIC: What is the bizarre link between the song 'Puff The Magic Dragon' and the Illinois Police Commission?

8 SCIENCE: What metal stays liquid over a greater range of temperature than any other?

9 THE ARTS: Which character appears in the most Shakespeare plays?

10 FILM, TV & RADIO: Who writes a weekly 'Letter From America'?

11 NATURAL HISTORY: Does a mosquito bite have anything to do with the insect's 47 teeth?

12 MISCELLANY: What is the rank above inspector in the British police?

▶ **QUIZMASTER:** After which film star did RAF airmen name a lifejacket?

ANSWERS 85

1 Clothes are less likely to tangle.

2 Bracknell, Berkshire.

3 Chartwell, Kent.

4 In a loudspeaker.

5 Canterbury Cathedral.

6 Henry Cooper's left hook.

7 Neil Diamond.

8 It is the rarest of the naturally occurring elements.

9 Simon Templar.

10 *Blood Simple*.

11 The flea (the equivalent of a human jumping about 375 yards).

12 The Charleston.

■ Butterflies.

ANSWERS 86

1 He falls off his board.

2 The Caribbean.

3 Mary Whitehouse.

4 A two-stage ring. (The whole ring, or just the inner part can be selected.)

5 1970.

6 Italy.

7 The commission included it in a blacklist of 'drug-orientated rock records' in 1971.

8 Gallium.

9 Falstaff.

10 Alistair Cooke.

11 No (it stings by means of a long proboscis).

12 Chief Inspector.

■ Mae West.

TRIVIA QUIZ 87

1 MISCELLANY: Which sport, apart from tennis, has its British headquarters at Wimbledon?

2 GEOGRAPHY & TRAVEL: Captain Cook left Britain and Count Dracula arrived via which town?

3 PEOPLE: Who lives at Lambeth Palace?

4 INVENTIONS: What is the self-adjusting device on a safety belt called?

5 HISTORY: What was the nickname of George, Prince of Wales, son of George III?

6 SPORT: Who won the World Drivers' Championship in 1975 and 1977?

7 MUSIC: Which letter-perfect group came up with an album called Lexicon of Love?

8 SCIENCE: What in astronomy is the red spot?

9 THE ARTS: Who was the detective hero of *The Big Sleep*?

10 FILM, TV & RADIO: In which 1972 film was Paul Newman almost upstaged by a beer-drinking bear?

11 NATURAL HISTORY: What bird was once believed to emerge from a barnacle, like a chicken from an egg?

12 MISCELLANY: What colour is the best vinho verde?

▶ **QUIZMASTER:** What is the origin of the 'soap' in 'soap opera'?

TRIVIA QUIZ 88

1 MISCELLANY: Which European nation is the cleanest (or at least consumes the most soap)?

2 GEOGRAPHY & TRAVEL: In which region of Italy are the Chianti Hills?

3 PEOPLE: Which Italianate village did Clough Williams-Ellis design in North Wales?

4 INVENTIONS: What is the chief characteristic of hydroponic cultivation of plants?

5 HISTORY: Which organisation did the UK join in 1973?

6 SPORT: Which two rugby union sides compete for the Calcutta Cup?

7 MUSIC: What was the first pop band to tour China?

8 SCIENCE: By what name is deoxyribonucleic acid better known?

9 THE ARTS: What kind of bird was Jonathan Livingston?

10 FILM, TV & RADIO: Ivy, Gail, Brian and Nicky share a surname. What is it?

11 NATURAL HISTORY: What is a prehensile tail?

12 MISCELLANY: What kind of animal is a schnauzer?

▶ **QUIZMASTER:** In what order, left to right, are the colours of the French flag?

ANSWERS 87

1 Croquet.

2 Whitby.

3 The Archbishop of Canterbury.

4 An inertia reel.

5 Prinny.

6 Niki Lauda.

7 ABC.

8 A storm that has been raging on Jupiter for several centuries.

9 Philip Marlow.

10 *The Life And Times Of Judge Roy Bean.*

11 The barnacle goose.

12 White.

■ Many of these type of programmes were originally sponsored by soap companies in the USA.

ANSWERS 88

1 Great Britain.

2 Tuscany.

3 Portmeirion.

4 They are grown without soil.

5 The EEC.

6 England and Scotland.

7 Wham!

8 DNA.

9 A seagull.

10 Tilsley (in *Coronation Street*).

11 A tail which can grip objects.

12 A dog.

■ Blue, white and red.

TRIVIA QUIZ 89

1 MISCELLANY: What is SALT an acronym for?

2 GEOGRAPHY & TRAVEL: Which is further North, Moscow or the Isle Of Skye?

3 PEOPLE: Who became leader of Iran in 1979?

4 INVENTIONS: How many hours a day does the average in-service jumbo jet fly?

5 HISTORY: Which English king was known as 'The Hammer of the Scots'?

6 SPORT: Which two sports are combined in a biathlon?

7 MUSIC: What was Rod Stewart's first hit?

8 SCIENCE: Which celebrated scientist was also a poet, musician, architect, sculptor, engineer and artist?

9 THE ARTS: Which French impressionist made his name with his depictions of ballet dancers?

10 FILM, TV & RADIO: Which character from *The Archers* thinks he is also a country and western star?

11 NATURAL HISTORY: Pica pica is the scientific name for what bird?

12 MISCELLANY: What sex was the person who cut Samson's hair?

▶ QUIZMASTER: How many times higher than Ayers Rock is Mont Blanc?

TRIVIA QUIZ 90

1 MISCELLANY: Who created the Metropolitan Police Force?

2 GEOGRAPHY & TRAVEL: In which American state is Mount St Helens?

3 PEOPLE: Who was the first member of the royal family to be interviewed on television?

4 INVENTIONS: Which common household gadget uses the same frequencies as radar?

5 HISTORY: Which American writer and lecturer was deaf and blind?

6 SPORT: Which sport has had these world champions: Lionel Van Praag of Australia, Jerzy Szczakiel of Poland, Ivan Mauger of New Zealand?

7 MUSIC: What was the name of Alison Moyet and Vince Clarke's group?

8 SCIENCE: In geology, what is Blue John?

9 THE ARTS: Which architect designed St Paul's Cathedral?

10 FILM, TV & RADIO: In which TV series did Clint Eastwood star?

11 NATURAL HISTORY: What is the difference between a leopard and a panther?

12 MISCELLANY: In which part of the mind, according to Freud, lies the conscience and sense of morality?

▶ QUIZMASTER: Who fell in love with Little White Dove?

ANSWERS 89

1 Strategic arms limitation talks.

2 The Isle Of Skye.

3 Ayatollah Khomeini.

4 10.

5 Edward I.

6 Skiing and shooting.

7 'Reason to Believe'.

8 Leonardo da Vinci.

9 Degas.

10 Eddie Grundy.

11 The magpie.

12 Male (Delilah called for a man to do it).

■ 15.

ANSWERS 90

1 Sir Robert Peel.

2 Washington State.

3 Prince Philip.

4 The microwave oven.

5 Helen Keller.

6 Speedway.

7 Yazoo.

8 A variety of a mineral known as fluorite (found in Castleton, Derbyshire).

9 Sir Christopher Wren.

10 *Rawhide*.

11 None.

12 The super-ego.

■ Running Bear (in the Johnny Preston song).

TRIVIA QUIZ 91

1 MISCELLANY: What is the correct name for Yugoslav plum brandy?

2 GEOGRAPHY & TRAVEL: Which is the world's biggest museum (in the area it covers)?

3 PEOPLE: Who led the Kon-Tiki expedition in 1947?

4 INVENTIONS: Which computer whizz-kid developed the C5 car?

5 HISTORY: What was the official residence of the British monarch before Buckingham Palace?

6 SPORT: Which bishop is a former England cricket captain?

7 MUSIC: Which Rhinestone Cowboy was a former Beach Boy?

8 SCIENCE: What was first used as an anaesthetic at St Bartholomew's Hospital in 1847?

9 THE ARTS: Which Shakespearean character has the most lines?

10 FILM, TV & RADIO: Which actress packed American cinemas that had never before shown a foreign film, with her debut performance in *And God Created Woman*?

11 NATURAL HISTORY: What is another name for a mavis?

12 MISCELLANY: By what other name do we usually refer to Norway lobsters, or Dublin Bay prawns?

▶ QUIZMASTER: Which civilisation instigated the seven-day week?

TRIVIA QUIZ 92

1 MISCELLANY: What catastrophe was caused by a shipment of Argentinian corned beef to Britain in 1964?

2 GEOGRAPHY & TRAVEL: In which city's harbour is The Little Mermaid?

3 PEOPLE: Who was the first British president of the European Commission?

4 INVENTIONS: Outside which government building were the first traffic lights used in 1868?

5 HISTORY: Who said 'Dr Livingstone, I presume?'

6 SPORT: Who was the BBC Sports Personality Of The Year in 1971?

7 MUSIC: Declan McManus is the real name of which star?

8 SCIENCE: What is ichthyology?

9 THE ARTS: Which English writer is reported to have been stabbed to death in a pub?

10 FILM, TV & RADIO: Who do *Brain Of Britain* and *Stop The Week* have in common?

11 NATURAL HISTORY: What are death caps?

12 MISCELLANY: What attracted eight and a half million people to Battersea Pleasure Gardens between May and September, 1951?

▶ QUIZMASTER: Where is the last battle scheduled to take place on the Day Of Judgement?

ANSWERS 91

1 Slivovitz.

2 The 23-acre New York Natural History Museum.

3 Thor Heyerdahl.

4 Sir Clive Sinclair.

5 St James' Palace.

6 The Rt. Rev. David Sheppard, Bishop of Liverpool.

7 Glen Campbell.

8 Chloroform.

9 Hamlet.

10 Brigitte Bardot.

11 Song thrush.

12 Scampi.

■ The Roman civilisation.

ANSWERS 92

1 An outbreak of typhoid (500 cases).

2 Copenhagen's.

3 Roy Jenkins.

4 The Houses Of Parliament.

5 Henry Stanley.

6 Princess Anne.

7 Elvis Costello.

8 The study of fishes.

9 Christopher Marlowe.

10 Robert Robinson.

11 A kind of poisonous fungi.

12 The Festival Of Britain.

■ Armageddon.

TRIVIA QUIZ 93

1 MISCELLANY: Why did the House Of Commons vote itself a day off on a June Wednesday in 1848?

2 GEOGRAPHY & TRAVEL: Where is the London Bridge which the current Thames bridge replaced?

3 PEOPLE: How long does the American president hold office?

4 INVENTIONS: Who said 'Come here Watson, I want you'?

5 HISTORY: Where was the last battle fought on English soil?

6 SPORT: Name two of the sports in which you 'boast'?

7 MUSIC: How many Jackson brothers are there?

8 SCIENCE: What is the name for the scientific study of human efficiency in working environments?

9 THE ARTS: Which novel features Major Major and Milo Minderbender?

10 FILM, TV & RADIO: To which country did Butch Cassidy and Sundance escape when things got too hot for them in the States?

11 NATURAL HISTORY: From which country did tulips originally come?

12 MISCELLANY: What did Amelia Earhart do before any other woman?

▶ **QUIZMASTER:** If a pop star was aged 33⅓ in '78, when was he born?

TRIVIA QUIZ 94

1 MISCELLANY: What is the Armenian religion?

2 GEOGRAPHY & TRAVEL: In which country is the fortress of Sacsahuamán?

3 PEOPLE: What do professional 'crammers' do?

4 INVENTIONS: What refinement of the wristwatch was patented by John Harwood in 1924?

5 HISTORY: Who fathered three successive English sovereigns?

6 SPORT: Who won seven Olympic swimming medals in 1972?

7 MUSIC: Which former Oxford University student and English literature teacher wrote 'Help Me Make It Through The Night'?

8 SCIENCE: What are the four Aristotelian elements?

9 THE ARTS: Which science fiction writer is also a fully qualified biochemist?

10 FILM, TV & RADIO: Spell the surname of the *Jim'll Fix It* presenter.

11 NATURAL HISTORY: What main characteristic distinguishes deciduous trees?

12 MISCELLANY: What do whales eat?

▶ **QUIZMASTER:** What is the furthest you can see on a clear day?

ANSWERS 93

1 To go to the Epsom Derby.

2 Arizona.

3 Four years.

4 Alexander Graham Bell (calling his assistant, the first message on the telephone).

5 Sedgemoor, Somerset.

6 Squash, real tennis, rackets and fives.

7 Six.

8 Ergonomics.

9 *Catch 22.*

10 Bolivia.

11 Turkey.

12 She flew the Atlantic.

■ In '45.

ANSWERS 94

1 Christianity.

2 Peru.

3 They give individual coaching for exams.

4 The first self-winding mechanism.

5 Henry VIII.

6 Mark Spitz.

7 Kris Kristofferson.

8 Air, earth, fire and water.

9 Isaac Asimov.

10 Savile.

11 They shed their leaves.

12 Krill.

■ About 93 million miles (the distance of the sun from the earth).

TRIVIA QUIZ 95

1 MISCELLANY: Where is Shangri-La hidden, according to the novelist James Hilton?

2 GEOGRAPHY & TRAVEL: What is the deepest cleft in the earth's surface on land?

3 PEOPLE: By what name is Robert Allen Zimmerman better known?

4 INVENTIONS: What is the name of a computer program that helps you perform calculations using rows of columns and figures?

5 HISTORY: What was the apostle Matthew's job?

6 SPORT: Name three of the four Grand Slam tennis tournaments.

7 MUSIC: What were New Order called before Ian Curtis died?

8 SCIENCE: What year was the first human heart transplant?

9 THE ARTS: Who had a dog called Gnasher?

10 FILM, TV & RADIO: Who played Blott in the television version of *Blott on the Landscape*?

11 NATURAL HISTORY: Which insect chews wood to make into a nest?

12 MISCELLANY: What is the name of the bell inside the clock tower at the Houses of Parliament?

▶ QUIZMASTER: What appreciation society calls its members 'The Sons Of The Desert'?

TRIVIA QUIZ 96

1 MISCELLANY: What do you call a three-line Japanese verse of five, seven and five syllables?

2 GEOGRAPHY & TRAVEL: Which city is dominated by Sugar Loaf Mountain?

3 PEOPLE: What are old boys of Winchester College called?

4 INVENTIONS: What was the significance of the arrival of Clipper Young America at Heathrow on January 22, 1970?

5 HISTORY: How long, to the nearest 50 years, has the calendar been used in its present form in England?

6 SPORT: Who was Young Cricketer Of The Year in 1963?

7 MUSIC: Who composed the album *Fans*?

8 SCIENCE: What vitamin was discovered in alfalfa and putrefying fishmeal in 1939?

9 THE ARTS: Who was Sir Percy Blakeney?

10 FILM, TV & RADIO: Who kept insisting he wasn't a number, but a free man?

11 NATURAL HISTORY: What are osiers?

12 MISCELLANY: What is *taedium vitae*?

▶ QUIZMASTER: Which loin of beef did Charles II insist on knighting because he liked it so much?

ANSWERS 95

1 In a Himalayan Valley.

2 The Grand Canyon.

3 Bob Dylan.

4 Spreadsheet.

5 He was a tax collector.

6 Wimbledon, the US, French and Australian championships.

7 Joy Division.

8 1967.

9 Dennis The Menace.

10 David Suchet.

11 The wasp.

12 Big Ben.

■ The Laurel And Hardy appreciation society.

ANSWERS 96

1 A haiku.

2 Rio de Janeiro.

3 Wykehamists.

4 It was the first scheduled passenger flight of the Boeing 747 (the Jumbo Jet).

5 Just over 230 years (since 1752).

6 Geoff Boycott.

7 Malcolm McLaren.

8 Vitamin K.

9 The Scarlet Pimpernel.

10 Patrick McGoohan in *The Prisoner*.

11 Slender branches of willow (used for basket weaving).

12 Weariness of life.

■ The sirloin.

TRIVIA QUIZ 97

1 MISCELLANY: What is a successful contract to win 12 tricks called in bridge?

2 GEOGRAPHY & TRAVEL: Near which town were Jaffa oranges first cultivated?

3 PEOPLE: What was Orville and Wilbur Wright's achievement in 1903?

4 INVENTIONS: At how many revolutions per minute does a long playing gramophone record turn?

5 HISTORY: Who founded the Girl Guides?

6 SPORT: What major sporting event took place at Sapporo, Japan in 1972?

7 MUSIC: Which group dropped £9,500 in pound notes on the heads of fans at a concert?

8 SCIENCE: What was the name of the first artificial satellite?

9 THE ARTS: What was Long John Silver's parrot called?

10 FILM, TV & RADIO: Which actor said his epitaph should read: 'He was lucky and he knew it'?

11 NATURAL HISTORY: What is a young kangaroo called?

12 MISCELLANY: What is 'Dutch' short for in the expression 'my old Dutch'?

▶ **QUIZMASTER:** The name of which poet is an anagram of toilets?

TRIVIA QUIZ 98

1 MISCELLANY: Which country first introduced compulsory primary education?

2 GEOGRAPHY & TRAVEL: Where is the headquarters of Interpol?

3 PEOPLE: How many years of marriage does a sapphire wedding celebrate?

4 INVENTIONS: What is the main component of glass?

5 HISTORY: When did Britain get its first Labour government?

6 SPORT: Ada Unsworth, Frank and Peggy Spencer and Ted Burroughs have all led winning teams on which televised competition?

7 MUSIC: What hairy creature did Dora Bryan want for Christmas in 1963?

8 SCIENCE: What common medical technique was first introduced to Britain from Turkey in 1721 and tried out on condemned criminals?

9 THE ARTS: Who was the leading conspirator in Shakespeare's *Julius Caesar*?

10 FILM, TV & RADIO: Where did the last scene of *The Graduate* take place?

11 NATURAL HISTORY: What is an eagle's nest called?

12 MISCELLANY: What was the most important royal ceremony Queen Victoria attended in 1838?

▶ **QUIZMASTER:** When did Mauretania abolish slavery?

ANSWERS 97

1 A little slam.

2 Jaffa, near Tel Aviv.

3 The first power-driven flight.

4 33⅓.

5 Robert Baden-Powell.

6 The Winter Olympics.

7 Steeleye Span.

8 Sputnick 1.

9 Captain Flint.

10 Cary Grant.

11 A joey.

12 Duchess.

■ T.S. Eliot.

ANSWERS 98

1 Germany.

2 Paris.

3 45.

4 Sand (quartz).

5 1924.

6 Formation dancing (on the BBC's *Come Dancing*).

7 A Beatle.

8 Inoculation.

9 Cassius.

10 On a bus.

11 An eyrie.

12 Her coronation.

■ 1981.

TRIVIA QUIZ 99

1 **MISCELLANY:** Which English royal palace did one critic call 'a collection of stone pumpkins and pepper pots'?

2 **GEOGRAPHY & TRAVEL:** In which ocean are the Galapagos Islands?

3 **PEOPLE:** Which manufacturing company was founded by Lord Nuffield?

4 **INVENTIONS:** What is the process called when milk is kept at 62°C for half an hour?

5 **HISTORY:** Where was Mary, Queen of Scots executed?

6 **SPORT:** What record did Beamon break at the 1968 Olympics?

7 **MUSIC:** What does the musical term *diminuendo* mean?

8 **SCIENCE:** Which has larger molecules, oil or water?

9 **THE ARTS:** Which playwright invented the name Wendy?

10 **FILM, TV & RADIO:** Scarecrows are bundles of straw dressed up as humans. Which human achieves a similar effect on TV by dressing up as a bundle of straw?

11 **NATURAL HISTORY:** What are young eels called?

12 **MISCELLANY:** What is a jampan?

▶ **QUIZMASTER:** How many metal rings are there within the numbers of a dart board?

TRIVIA QUIZ 100

1 **MISCELLANY:** Who was U.S. President during the depression?

2 **GEOGRAPHY & TRAVEL:** Which city does the Liffey flow through?

3 **PEOPLE:** Who succeeded the Queen Mother as Chancellor of London University?

4 **INVENTIONS:** Who invented the alloy pinchbeck?

5 **HISTORY:** Which Carthaginian general defeated the Romans after an epic mountain march?

6 **SPORT:** Name the home city of one of these baseball teams: The Red Sox, The Yankees, The Cardinals.

7 **MUSIC:** What song by Dire Straits' Mark Knopfler was inspired by seeing a second-rate jazz band in a pub at Greenwich?

8 **SCIENCE:** What does iron become when a little carbon is added?

9 **THE ARTS:** Which book written by Edith Holden became a best-seller recently, well after her death?

10 **FILM, TV & RADIO:** Who became an actor after being dismissed from a Marks and Spencer training scheme because of his outrageous clothes?

11 **NATURAL HISTORY:** What are cone-bearing trees called?

12 **MISCELLANY:** What are the following: pig, craps and Everest?

▶ **QUIZMASTER:** Which well-known character also operates under the following names: Old Harry, Clootie and Auld Hornie?

ANSWERS 99

1 Brighton Pavilion.

2 The Pacific Ocean.

3 Morris Motors.

4 Pasteurization.

5 Fotheringay Castle.

6 The long jump record.

7 Gradually decreasing in volume.

8 Oil.

9 J.M. Barrie (in *Peter Pan*).

10 Jon Pertwee.

11 Elvers.

12 A type of sedan chair used in India.

■ Six.

ANSWERS 100

1 Franklin D. Roosevelt.

2 Dublin.

3 Princess Anne.

4 Thomas Pinchbeck.

5 Hannibal.

6 The Red Sox – Boston, The Yankees – New York, The Cardinals – St Louis

7 'Sultans Of Swing'.

8 Steel.

9 *The Country Diary Of An Edwardian Lady*.

10 Edward Fox.

11 Conifers.

12 They are all dice games.

■ The Devil.

TRIVIA QUIZ 101

1 MISCELLANY: How many squares are there on a draughts board?

2 GEOGRAPHY & TRAVEL: In which American state is San Antonio?

3 PEOPLE: Who did James Earl Ray murder in 1968?

4 INVENTIONS: Can computers play chess better than humans?

5 HISTORY: Where was Prime Minister Spencer Perceval assassinated?

6 SPORT: Who were the first winners of the European Cup in football?

7 MUSIC: Which Greek composer has a studio near Marble Arch called Nemo?

8 SCIENCE: What disease was first encountered at the Siege of Mecca in 569?

9 THE ARTS: What was won by John Steinbeck in 1962 and Sir Winston Churchill in 1953?

10 FILM, TV & RADIO: What song did Hal sing in *2001*?

11 NATURAL HISTORY: How many muscles, to the nearest ten, do you use when you make one forward step?

12 MISCELLANY: What is a shakuhachi?

▶ QUIZMASTER: What 28-year task did Dr Robert Burchfield complete in 1985, with the word Zyrian?

TRIVIA QUIZ 102

1 MISCELLANY: By what name is the skeleton dug up at Piltdown, Sussex in 1912 (later found to be an elaborate hoax) known?

2 GEOGRAPHY & TRAVEL: Where is Ruritania?

3 PEOPLE: In what business did William Randolph Hearst succeed?

4 INVENTIONS: What is plastic and coated with a film of magnetic iron oxide one ten-thousandth of an inch thick?

5 HISTORY: Who sailed from Spain in the *Santa Maria* in 1492?

6 SPORT: Which football team won the First Division Championship twice in the 1970s, but is now in the third division?

7 MUSIC: What instrument introduces *Rhapsody In Blue*?

8 SCIENCE: In which science would you expect to come across the Witch of Agnesi?

9 THE ARTS: Which famous painter was portrayed on screen by Kirk Douglas?

10 FILM, TV & RADIO: Which song and dance star of British musicals became Mrs Dale on radio?

11 NATURAL HISTORY: Where did turkeys originate?

12 MISCELLANY: What nationality was Edvard Munch?

▶ QUIZMASTER: What would happen to you if you were defenestrated?

ANSWERS 101

1 64.

2 Texas.

3 Martin Luther King.

4 No.

5 The lobby of The House Of Commons.

6 Real Madrid.

7 Vangelis.

8 Smallpox.

9 The Nobel Prize for Literature.

10 'Daisy, Daisy'.

11 54.

12 A Japanese flute.

■ Updating of the *Oxford English Dictionary*.

ANSWERS 102

1 Piltdown Man.

2 Nowhere – it is the imaginary country created by Anthony Hope for his novels *The Prisoner of Zenda* and *Rupert of Hentzau*.

3 Newspaper publishing.

4 Magnetic tape.

5 Christopher Columbus.

6 Derby County.

7 The clarinet.

8 Mathematics.

9 Van Gogh.

10 Jessie Matthews.

11 North America.

12 Norwegian.

■ You would be thrown out of a window.

TRIVIA QUIZ 103

1 MISCELLANY: Which pop star once recorded the *Crossroads* theme music?

2 GEOGRAPHY & TRAVEL: Of which country is Khartoum the capital?

3 PEOPLE: Which country had the world's first woman prime minister?

4 INVENTIONS: What was the profession of Dick Derrick, after whom the Derrick crane was named?

5 HISTORY: Which London airport site was once a race track?

6 SPORT: What kind of game is Aunt Sally?

7 MUSIC: Who is the gifted daughter of the Reverend C.L. Franklin?

8 SCIENCE: What differentiates a ferrous alloy from a non-ferrous alloy?

9 THE ARTS: What was the surname of the sisters in *Little Women*?

10 FILM, TV & RADIO: Which TV drama showed the effect of a nuclear bomb falling on Sheffield?

11 NATURAL HISTORY: What bird family does the bunting belong to?

12 MISCELLANY: What is the meaning of the Cockney rhyming slang expression deriving from Scapa Flow?

▶ QUIZMASTER: What were originally known in Britain as 'love-apples'?

TRIVIA QUIZ 104

1 MISCELLANY What is an Australian bushman's 'Matilda'?

2 GEOGRAPHY & TRAVEL: Where is Wall Street?

3 PEOPLE: Who or what is a cartographer?

4 INVENTIONS: Why is lead added to petrol?

5 HISTORY: Bangladesh became independent in 1971. What was it called before that date?

6 SPORT: Who won the World Professional Snooker Championship 15 times between 1927 and 1946?

7 MUSIC: Which Jewish American singer became a Born Again Christian in 1979?

8 SCIENCE: Why is Goldbach's Conjecture not called a 'theory'?

9 THE ARTS: Who succeeded Lorenz Hart as lyricist to Richard Rodgers?

10 FILM, TV & RADIO: Who was the host of *Take Your Pick*?

11 NATURAL HISTORY: Which plant is processed for linseed oil?

12 MISCELLANY: Which TV show was compered by a frog?

▶ QUIZMASTER: What enduring burden did William Pitt The Younger impose on Britain in 1799?

ANSWERS 103

1 Paul McCartney.

2 The Sudan.

3 Ceylon (Mrs Bandaranaike).

4 A hangman.

5 Gatwick.

6 A funfair game in which sticks or balls are thrown at the mouth of a wooden figure.

7 Aretha Franklin.

8 Ferrous alloys contain iron.

9 March.

10 *Threads*.

11 The finch family.

12 Go (Scapa Flow = go, probably also the origin of the slang word scarper).

■ Tomatoes.

ANSWERS 104

1 His pack or swag.

2 New York.

3 Someone who draws maps.

4 To reduce engine knock.

5 East Pakistan.

6 Joe Davis.

7 Bob Dylan.

8 Because nobody has been able to prove it. (That any even number can be expressed as the sum of two prime numbers.)

9 Oscar Hammerstein.

10 Michael Miles.

11 Flax.

12 *The Muppets*.

■ Income Tax.

TRIVIA QUIZ 105

1 MISCELLANY: What liquid is brandy distilled from?

2 GEOGRAPHY & TRAVEL: Which city would you reach by phone from London if you dialled the code 031?

3 PEOPLE: Who was the first president of independent Kenya in 1964?

4 INVENTIONS: Who was Britain's first telephone subscriber?

5 HISTORY: Which famous soldier was assassinated while sailing round the coast of Ireland?

6 SPORT: What is the lowest weight category in boxing?

7 MUSIC: What is Abba an acronym for?

8 SCIENCE: Which metal has the symbol Au?

9 THE ARTS: Who wrote the lyrics of *Starlight Express* to Andrew Lloyd-Webber's music?

10 FILM, TV & RADIO: What was TW3?

11 NATURAL HISTORY: What is a fox's tail called?

12 MISCELLANY: In chess, how many squares does a king move in a castling manoeuvre?

▶ **QUIZMASTER:** What group took its name from a line by William Blake?

TRIVIA QUIZ 106

1 MISCELLANY: What is a marmite?

2 GEOGRAPHY & TRAVEL: What was the natural disaster that killed four people and damaged 1,200 buildings in the Colchester area on April 22, 1884?

3 PEOPLE: What does The Soviet Union call its supreme policy-making body?

4 INVENTIONS: By what process is chromium applied to car parts?

5 HISTORY: What did Mary Baker Eddy found in the late 1800s?

6 SPORT: What is the name for the waterproof trousers with bib worn by skiiers?

7 MUSIC: What piece of operatic music accompanies the transformation of a Russian prince into a vengeful insect?

8 SCIENCE: Ursa Minor is the name of a group of stars. What does it mean?

9 THE ARTS: What is the second book of *The Bible*?

10 FILM, TV & RADIO: Which chat show host flirted with Miss Piggy and was floored by Emu?

11 NATURAL HISTORY: What mammal can endure temperatures below freezing while it is in hibernation?

12 MISCELLANY: In his will, who left his second best bed to his wife?

▶ **QUIZMASTER:** Which star in his 50s still has a curvaceous figure and averages 15 costume changes a night during live performances?

ANSWERS 105

1 Wine.

2 Edinburgh.

3 Jomo Kenyatta.

4 Queen Victoria (she asked Alexander Graham Bell for a pair of telephones in 1878).

5 Earl Mountbatten of Burma.

6 Light flyweight.

7 The names of the group members (Agnetha, Benny, Bjorn and Anni-Frid).

8 Gold.

9 Richard Stilgoe.

10 *That Was The Week That Was* (a 1960s satirical show hosted by David Frost).

11 A brush.

12 Two.

■ The Doors.

ANSWERS 106

1 An earthenware cooking pot.

2 An eathquake.

3 The Politburo.

4 Electroplating.

5 The Christian Science movement.

6 A sallopette.

7 *The Flight Of The Bumble Bee.*

8 Little Bear.

9 Exodus.

10 Michael Parkinson.

11 The bat.

12 William Shakespeare.

■ Danny La Rue.

1 MISCELLANY: Where on a cheque is the sorting code printed?

2 GEOGRAPHY & TRAVEL: Where is the town of Tequila?

3 PEOPLE: What is Britain's largest trade union?

4 INVENTIONS: What did Samuel Morse invent in 1884?

5 HISTORY: What creature did early Christians use as a symbol of Christ?

6 SPORT: To what kind of horse do The Oaks and The 1,000 Guineas restrict themselves?

7 MUSIC: Who took over from Bob Neal as Elvis Presley's manager?

8 If you beamed an alpha ray towards a row of materials in this order — a sheet of paper, a one inch piece of wood, a sheet of glass and a panel of lead — which would stop it?

9 THE ARTS: Whose first novel was *The Man Within*?

10 FILM, TV & RADIO: What planet did *Star Trek's* Dr Spock come from?

11 NATURAL HISTORY: What is a herbivore?

12 MISCELLANY: What is a novella?

▶ **QUIZMASTER:** Who said 'Men seldom make passes at girls who wear glasses'?

TRIVIA QUIZ 108

1 MISCELLANY: What is the flavouring in ouzo?

2 GEOGRAPHY & TRAVEL: In which country did the samba originate?

3 PEOPLE: What was the name of the car in which Donald Campbell broke the land speed record?

4 INVENTIONS: What was the German Hans Joachim von Ohain the first to put into practice, narrowly beating Englishman Frank Whittle?

5 HISTORY: Who was the first member of the British royal family to be killed while flying on active service?

6 SPORT: Which woman athlete won Britain a silver medal at the Mexico Olympics but subsequently died of cancer?

7 MUSIC: Which group did Paul Weller form after The Jam?

8 SCIENCE: Where in Britain was the first combined heart and lung transplant operation performed?

9 THE ARTS: Who shot himself mortally in the mouth in Idaho in 1961?

10 FILM, TV & RADIO: Who played Henry Crun, Lance Brigadier Grytpype-Thynne and Bluebottle?

11 NATURAL HISTORY: What is caviar?

12 MISCELLANY: Who sang 'Hope I die before I get old' and learned to live with it?

▶ **QUIZMASTER:** 'To extract a tenth from' is a definition of which verb?

ANSWERS 107

1 The top right hand corner.

2 Mexico

3 The Transport And General Workers' Union.

4 The morse code.

5 A fish.

6 Fillies.

7 Colonel Tom Parker.

8 The sheet of paper.

9 Graham Greene's.

10 Vulcan.

11 An animal with a plant diet.

12 A short novel.

■ Dorothy Parker.

ANSWERS 108

1 Aniseed.

2 Brazil.

3 *Bluebird*.

4 The jet engine.

5 The Duke Of Kent in 1942.

6 Lilian Board.

7 The Style Council.

8 Harefield Hospital, in December 1983.

9 Ernest Hemingway.

10 Peter Sellers (in *The Goons*).

11 The roe of a fish (usually the sturgeon).

12 Roger Daltrey.

■ Decimate.

TRIVIA QUIZ 109

1 MISCELLANY: What do the initials OPEC stand for?

2 GEOGRAPHY & TRAVEL: What is a coral island with a curved reef enclosing a lagoon called?

3 PEOPLE: What do Americans call nappies?

4 INVENTIONS: Which artist first sketched out the principle of the parachute?

5 HISTORY: Which outlaw's real name was William Bonney?

6 SPORT: Who was the champion jockey in flat racing for the four years from 1974 – 1977?

7 MUSIC: What is the First Post, if it comes at 9.30pm?

8 SCIENCE: Why is carbon dioxide put in certain types of fire extinguishers?

9 THE ARTS: In which book did *The Hispaniola* feature?

10 FILM, TV & RADIO: What is the family link connecting *Dallas* and the King Of Rock 'n' Roll?

11 NATURAL HISTORY: What disease has been used to control the rabbit population?

12 MISCELLANY: In which city was the Communist party set up in 1848?

▶ QUIZMASTER: The name of which particle, when translated from the Greek, means 'cannot be cut'?

TRIVIA QUIZ 110

1 MISCELLANY: With what metal did the alchemists associate Mars?

2 GEOGRAPHY & TRAVEL: What is the main product of the Jura Mountain region and the valley of the Aar, Switzerland?

3 PEOPLE: Who established the modern theory of biological evolution?

4 INVENTIONS: What did Léon Gaumont produce for the first time in France before 1900?

5 HISTORY: What route linked Canterbury and Winchester in medieval times?

6 SPORT: Which famous rugby player was also a Wimbledon junior tennis champion?

7 MUSIC: Which rock 'n' roller and his son Ricky, wrote a string of hit songs for his daughter?

8 SCIENCE: What is the Latin name for the Polar Star?

9 THE ARTS: Whose daughters were Regan, Goneril and Cordelia?

10 FILM, TV & RADIO: Which singing duo found fame and recognition via a TV beer advertisement?

11 NATURAL HISTORY: What are cavicorns?

12 MISCELLANY: What is dried, wild marjoram called?

▶ QUIZMASTER: What Antipodean wonder did Londoners flock to the Lyceum Theatre in The Strand to see for the first time in 1791?

ANSWERS 109

1 The Organisation of Petroleum Exporting Countries.

2 An atoll.

3 Diapers.

4 Leonardo da Vinci.

5 Billy The Kid.

6 Pat Eddery.

7 A British Army bugle call.

8 To stop electrical fires (it does not conduct electricity).

9 Treasure Island.

10 Elvis Presley's widow Priscilla plays Jenna Wade in *Dallas*.

11 Myxomatosis.

12 London.

■ The atom.

ANSWERS 110

1 Iron.

2 Clocks and watches.

3 Charles Darwin.

4 Talking films. (They were synchronised to gramophone records).

5 The Pilgrim's Way.

6 JPR Williams.

7 Marty Wilde for Kim Wilde.

8 Polaris.

9 King Lear's.

10 Chas and Dave with 'Gertcha'.

11 Animals with hollow horns.

12 Oregano.

■ The first imported live kangaroo.

TRIVIA QUIZ 111

1 **MISCELLANY:** Sugar, water and white of egg were the only ingredients of what popular Victorian children's treat?

2 **GEOGRAPHY & TRAVEL:** Which loch lies closest to Glasgow?

3 **PEOPLE:** What was Jacqueline (Kennedy) Onassis' maiden name?

4 **INVENTIONS:** Who sent the first radio telegraph signal across the Atlantic?

5 **HISTORY:** Who was the first Plantagenet king?

6 **SPORT:** What much-reported occurrence interrupted Bill Beaumont's half-time team talk at Twickenham in 1981?

7 **MUSIC:** Name the band of Vince de la Cruz, Kimberley Rew, Alex Cooper and Katrina Leskaniel.

8 **SCIENCE:** How is the Common Business Oriented Language commonly referred to in computing?

9 **THE ARTS:** Which best-selling author once represented Louth in Parliament?

10 **FILM, TV & RADIO:** Which former sex symbol starred in *Bittersweet Love* in 1976?

11 **NATURAL HISTORY:** What is the medical name for the shoulder blade?

12 **MISCELLANY:** What kind of plant is peyote?

▶ **QUIZMASTER:** What, according to Edward Young and headmasters the world over, is the 'thief of time'?

TRIVIA QUIZ 112

1 **MISCELLANY:** Which minister lives at 11 Downing Street?

2 **GEOGRAPHY & TRAVEL:** Where is Robin Hood's Bay?

3 **PEOPLE:** Who carried out the first manned orbit of the earth?

4 **INVENTIONS:** What kind of boat, invented in 1898, is held clear of the water by underwater wings?

5 **HISTORY:** What do the Albert Memorial and St Pancras Station have in common?

6 **SPORT:** In 1984 which country wrested the Americas Cup away from the United States?

7 **MUSIC:** Which Bach compositions were never performed for the nobleman to whom they were dedicated?

8 **SCIENCE:** The Earth doesn't take exactly 24 hours to rotate. Is it faster or slower?

9 **THE ARTS:** Whose is the first Canterbury tale?

10 **FILM, TV & RADIO:** Who played the title role in *The Elephant Man*?

11 **NATURAL HISTORY:** What is a fox's den called?

12 **MISCELLANY:** What is another name for the drug Drinamyl and also a medal awarded to wounded US servicemen?

▶ **QUIZMASTER:** Which Bohemian ruler, featured in a popular translation of a Czechoslovakian carol, was murdered by his brother?

ANSWERS 111

1 Barley sugar.

2 Loch Lomond.

3 Bouvier.

4 Marconi.

5 Henry II.

6 Erica Rowe's streak.

7 Katrina and the Waves.

8 COBOL.

9 Jeffrey Archer.

10 Lana Turner.

11 The scapula.

12 Cactus.

■ Procrastination.

ANSWERS 112

1 The Chancellor of the Exchequer.

2 North Yorkshire.

3 John Glenn.

4 The hydrofoil.

5 The same architect (Sir George Gilbert Scott).

6 Australia.

7 The Brandenburg Concertos. (They were dedicated to the Margrave of Brandenburg.)

8 Faster (23 hours, 56 minutes, 4.09 seconds).

9 The knight's.

10 John Hurt.

11 An earth.

12 Purple Heart.

■ Good King Wenceslas.

TRIVIA QUIZ 113

1 MISCELLANY: What is the US Defence Department headquarters building called?

2 GEOGRAPHY & TRAVEL: Which city was faced with a $1 billion debt after staging the Olympic Games?

3 PEOPLE: Which organisation has the motto 'Blood And Fire'?

4 INVENTIONS: James Hargreaves' invention revolutionized the cotton textiles industry. What was it?

5 HISTORY: Which monarch bought the estate of Sandringham?

6 SPORT: To whom did Alan Minter lose his world title?

7 MUSIC: Who died in the back of a powder blue cadillac on New Year's day 1953?

8 SCIENCE: What did the Austrian Government sell in 1909 at £10,000 for a single gramme?

9 THE ARTS: What book about a horse was written by the Victorian Anna Sewell?

10 FILM, TV & RADIO: What actress and singer is part Armenian, part Red Indian, a former Ronette and a Vogue model?

11 NATURAL HISTORY: Where in the garden would you find rhizomes and tubers?

12 MISCELLANY: What colour is a palomino horse?

▶ **QUIZMASTER:** What was the name of the previous £1 coin.

TRIVIA QUIZ 114

1 MISCELLANY: What does a phillumenist collect?

2 GEOGRAPHY & TRAVEL: In which town did Albert Spaggiari carry out the world's biggest bank robbery?

3 PEOPLE: What do the ailurophobic fear?

4 INVENTIONS: What is glass fibre made out of?

5 HISTORY: How did Sir Thomas More die?

6 SPORT: What is the last event in the decathlon?

7 MUSIC: What orchestral work did Sibelius write as a patriotic tribute to his homeland?

8 SCIENCE: What everyday element is 755 times heavier than air?

9 THE ARTS: Which poet died off the Italian coast at the age of 30?

10 FILM, TV & RADIO: Why is Anthony Perkins strictly speaking 'not guilty' of the shower scene murder in Hitchcock's *Psycho*?

11 NATURAL HISTORY: Which carries blood to the heart, veins or arteries?

12 MISCELLANY: What is the unique capability of the knight in chess, apart from its L-shaped motion?

▶ **QUIZMASTER:** Which of two clocks is more accurate: one which loses a minute a day or one which doesn't work at all?

ANSWERS 113

1 The Pentagon, Washington.

2 Montreal.

3 The Salvation Army.

4 The spinning jenny.

5 Queen Victoria.

6 Marvin Hagler.

7 Hank Williams.

8 Radium.

9 *Black Beauty*.

10 Cher.

11 Underground. (They're stems of plants).

12 Golden with a cream or white mane and tail.

■ The sovereign.

ANSWERS 114

1 Matchbox labels.

2 Nice.

3 Cats.

4 Glass (in very fine strands).

5 He was beheaded (for treason).

6 The 1,500 metres.

7 *Finlandia*.

8 Water.

9 Shelley.

10 He wasn't on the set at the time (a stand-in played the knifeman).

11 Veins.

12 It can jump other pieces.

■ The one which does not work because it's right twice daily.

TRIVIA QUIZ 115

1 MISCELLANY: What is the pattern of notes in Hindu music which provides the basis for improvisation?

2 GEOGRAPHY & TRAVEL: Which is the largest of the Scilly Isles?

3 PEOPLE: Where is the ancient winter game of shinty played?

4 INVENTIONS: What is frozen carbon dioxide better known as?

5 HISTORY: What crime did Burke and Hare commit?

6 SPORT: What in golf, is the name given for two under par for the hole?

7 MUSIC: What is a paradiddle?

8 SCIENCE: What is the name given to an optical illusion caused by unusual atmospheric conditions?

9 THE ARTS: Which family's life story formed the basis for *The Sound Of Music*?

10 FILM, TV & RADIO: Who is Betty in *A Private Function*?

11 NATURAL HISTORY: What is Britain's largest freshwater fish?

12 MISCELLANY: What is a putsch?

▶ *The Underground Executioner* is the title of the favourite soap opera of which nation?

TRIVIA QUIZ 116

1 MISCELLANY: Who introduced the Christmas tree to England from Bavaria?

2 GEOGRAPHY & TRAVEL: What term is used to describe the warm front of a depression being overtaken by its cold front?

3 PEOPLE: Which country has Robert Mugabe as prime minister?

4 INVENTIONS: In which country was paper first used?

5 HISTORY: Who said 'Religion is the opium of the people'?

6 SPORT: Where were the Olympic Games held in 1972?

7 MUSIC: Who did Jimi Hendrix once praise on the Jimmy Carson TV show as one of America's most promising guitarists?

8 SCIENCE: During which month is the earth nearest the sun?

9 THE ARTS: 'The Kiss' is probably the best known sculpture in a British gallery. Who is it by?

10 FILM, TV & RADIO: Which mother and daughter superstars were both coached by Kay Thompson?

11 NATURAL HISTORY: Which bird has plumes on its head resembling the quills secretaries used to put behind their ears?

12 MISCELLANY: Which child hero did Anthony Buckeridge create in 1948?

▶ QUIZMASTER: Under what circumstances can Rue de la Paix, Schlossallée, Boardwalk and Mayfair be found at the same location?

ANSWERS 115

1 A raga.

2 St Mary's.

3 The Scottish Highlands.

4 Dry ice.

5 Body-snatching and murder (they sold their victims' bodies for medical research).

6 An eagle.

7 A drum roll.

8 A mirage.

9 The Von Trapps.

10 A pig.

11 The pike.

12 A revolution attempt.

■ Japan.

ANSWERS 116

1 Prince Albert.

2 An occlusion.

3 Zimbabwe.

4 China (in AD 105).

5 Karl Marx.

6 Munich.

7 Billy Gibbons of ZZ Top, then a member of The Moving Sidewalks.

8 January.

9 Auguste Rodin.

10 Judy Garland and Liza Minnelli.

11 The secretary bird.

12 Jennings.

■ On Monopoly boards (of France, Germany, America and England respectively).

TRIVIA QUIZ 117

1 MISCELLANY: What is the name of the rules governing British boxing?

2 GEOGRAPHY & TRAVEL: What is a ria?

3 PEOPLE: Which county's villages still follow the old custom of 'well-dressing'?

4 INVENTIONS: What was the first plastic material to be manufactured?

5 HISTORY: Who was the last king to be crowned in Scotland?

6 SPORT: Name one of the athletes celebrated in the film *Chariots Of Fire*.

7 MUSIC: Which celebratory song was written by music publisher Clayton F. Summy and plagiarised by Stravinsky?

8 SCIENCE: What explosive was first tested at Lydd, Sussex in 1888?

9 THE ARTS: Who invented Utopia?

10 FILM, TV & RADIO: What is the name of Yogi Bear's side-kick?

11 NATURAL HISTORY: What is the medical name for the wind pipe?

12 MISCELLANY: Which chancellor of the last ten years was accused of taxing fish and chips?

▶ QUIZMASTER: When the rate of inflation is going down, does it mean that prices are rising, falling or staying the same?

TRIVIA QUIZ 118

1 MISCELLANY: What, apart from a rude name, do you call an invoice which arrives before the goods?

2 GEOGRAPHY & TRAVEL: What is a tremor on the moon's surface called?

3 PEOPLE: What was the British nickname for William Joyce, the broadcaster of World War II?

4 INVENTIONS: What device is Isaac Merritt Singer famous for?

5 HISTORY: What did the Combination Act forbid?

6 SPORT: What did Kennington Oval become during World War II?

7 MUSIC: Which World War II fanfare by Aaron Copland was a 1977 hit for Emerson, Lake and Palmer?

8 SCIENCE: What was the last planet to be discovered?

9 THE ARTS: How many brothers Karamazov were there?

10 FILM, TV & RADIO: What is the colour of Mr Spock's blood?

11 NATURAL HISTORY: How many bones are there in the human body, to the nearest 20?

12 MISCELLANY: What is the oldest form of drama in Japan?

▶ QUIZMASTER: What is the estimated average annual wage of a starring role in *Dynasty*: £100,000, £400,000, £750,000, £1,000,000?

ANSWERS 117

1 The Queensbury Rules.

2 A flooded river valley.

3 Derbyshire's.

4 Celluloid (in 1868).

5 Charles II.

6 Harold Abrahams and Eric Liddell.

7 'Happy Birthday To You'.

8 Lyddite.

9 Sir Thomas More.

10 Boo Boo.

11 The trachea.

12 Nigel Lawson. (He put VAT on take-away foods.)

■ Rising.

ANSWERS 118

1 A pro-forma invoice.

2 A moonquake.

3 Lord Haw-Haw.

4 The Singer sewing machine.

5 The formation of trade unions.

6 A prisoner of war camp.

7 'Fanfare For The Common Man'.

8 Pluto (in 1930).

9 Four.

10 Green.

11 206.

12 Noh.

■ *Dynasty* stars are reputed to be paid more than one million pounds a year.

TRIVIA QUIZ 119

1 MISCELLANY: Which ministerial post has a higher salary than the Prime Minister's?

2 GEOGRAPHY & TRAVEL: In which country will you find Quechuan Indians?

3 PEOPLE: Which politician is best remembered as the architect of the National Health Service?

4 INVENTIONS: Where was the first glass made?

5 HISTORY: Which military commander won the victories of Blenheim, Ramilles, Oudenarde and Malplaquet?

6 SPORT: What is the letter K worth in Scrabble?

7 MUSIC: What did the Tennessee radio Programme WSM Barndance change its name to?

8 SCIENCE: What is an orrery?

9 THE ARTS: Which poet died on an American lecture tour at the age of 39?

10 FILM, TV & RADIO: What was the name of the hospital where Dr Kildare worked?

11 NATURAL HISTORY: What is the popular name for the crane fly?

12 MISCELLANY: What consumer durable will you find in 96.6% of British households?

▶ QUIZMASTER: What does spago mean in Italian?

TRIVIA QUIZ 120

1 MISCELLANY: The life expectation of a British man in 1901 was 49. What is it today?

2 GEOGRAPHY & TRAVEL: Which islands are further north, the Shetlands or the Faeroes?

3 PEOPLE: What do vulcanologists study?

4 INVENTIONS: What was the first metal used by man?

5 HISTORY: Hadrian's Wall marked the northern boundary of which empire?

6 SPORT: Under what circumstances did Lord Castlereagh wound George Canning in 1809?

7 MUSIC: Who is Vincent Furnier more commonly known as?

8 SCIENCE: What is the alternative name for X-rays?

9 THE ARTS: Which poet died of self-administered arsenic at the age of 17?

10 FILM, TV & RADIO: Who left *Dynasty* to star in a movie which she co-wrote, called *Torchlight*?

11 NATURAL HISTORY: How many pints of air does the average adult breathe in a year, to the nearest million?

12 MISCELLANY: How many players in solo whist?

▶ QUIZMASTER: Which particular word, advised Julie Andrews, is a panacea in most circumstances?

ANSWERS 119

1 The Lord Chancellor.

2 Peru.

3 Aneurin Bevan.

4 Egypt.

5 The Duke of Marlborough.

6 5.

7 *The Grand Ole Opry.*

8 A mechanical model that reproduces the movements of the planets.

9 Dylan Thomas.

10 Blair General.

11 Daddy Longlegs.

12 The television.

■ String.

ANSWERS 120

1 70.

2 The Faeroes.

3 Volcanoes.

4 Copper.

5 The Roman Empire.

6 They were having a duel.

7 Alice Cooper.

8 Röntgen rays.

9 Thomas Chatterton.

10 Pamela Sue Martin.

11 Nearly eight million.

12 Four.

■ 'Supercalifragilisticexpialidocious'.

TRIVIA QUIZ 121

1 **MISCELLANY:** What does R & B stand for?

2 **GEOGRAPHY & TRAVEL:** What is the world's largest trading block?

3 **PEOPLE:** Who retired as General Secretary of the TUC in 1984?

4 **INVENTIONS:** In what object might you find a mixture of potassium nitrate, gunpowder, sulphur and aluminium dust, among other things?

5 **HISTORY:** Who was the only English pope?

6 **SPORT:** What sporting event took place in Helsinki in 1952?

7 **MUSIC:** What song was Julie Burchill talking about when she said it was: 'the nearest yet that a pop record has come to committing a war crime'?

8 **SCIENCE:** Why do space rockets have to travel at a minimum speed of seven miles a second on take-off?

9 **THE ARTS:** What breed of dog is Snoopy?

10 **FILM, TV & RADIO:** Who directed *The Effect Of Gamma Rays On Man-In-The-Moon Marigolds?*

11 **NATURAL HISTORY:** What in human beings is the tube which carries food to the stomach?

12 **MISCELLANY:** What was unique about the appointment in 1985 of Paul Reeves as Governor-General of New Zealand?

▶ **QUIZMASTER:** Where was the first British Women's Institute founded?

TRIVIA QUIZ 122

1 **MISCELLANY:** What do you call the offspring of a tiger and a lioness?

2 **GEOGRAPHY & TRAVEL:** Where do Geordies live?

3 **PEOPLE:** Which writer has the longest entry in *Who's Who*?

4 **INVENTIONS:** What was the name of the advanced rocket weapon the Germans fired at London during World War II?

5 **HISTORY:** Who crossed the Rubicon to invade Italy?

6 **SPORT:** What is the name of the inter-island cricket trophy that forms the basis of first class cricket in the West Indies?

7 **MUSIC:** Who said 'What'd I Say'?

8 **SCIENCE:** What was the name of the stone that was supposed to turn lead into gold?

9 **THE ARTS:** Who wrote a poem about a 'mystery cat'?

10 **FILM, TV & RADIO:** Which cop show, after a disastrous first series, went on to top the ratings?

11 **NATURAL HISTORY:** What was the archaeopteryx the first creature to do?

12 **MISCELLANY:** What is an aulete?

 QUIZMASTER: If you tear a piece of paper in half and put the two pieces on top of each other, tear them across again, then repeat the process 50 times, how high will your pile of paper be: 15 feet, 200 yards, 17 million miles?

ANSWERS 121

1 Rhythm And Blues.

2 The EEC.

3 Len Murray.

4 A firework.

5 Nicholas Breakspear, who became Pope Adrian IV.

6 The Olympic Games.

7 '19' (by Paul Hardcastle).

8 In order to escape the Earth's atmosphere.

9 A beagle.

10 Paul Newman.

11 The oesophagus.

12 He was the first Maori to hold the post.

■ Llanfairpwllgwyngyllgogerychwy-rndrobwllllantysiliogogogoch (a spirited attempt at this will do).

ANSWERS 122

1 A Tigon.

2 Tyneside.

3 Barbara Cartland.

4 The VI (or V2).

5 Julius Caesar.

6 The Shell Shield.

7 Ray Charles.

8 The Philosopher's Stone.

9 T.S. Eliot.

10 *Hill Street Blues*.

11 Fly.

12 A flute player.

■ About 17 million miles, though most people give up before they get that far.

TRIVIA QUIZ 123

1 MISCELLANY: Which female star did Laurence Olivier describe as 'a professional amateur'?

2 GEOGRAPHY & TRAVEL: What is Britain's most heavily populated dependency?

3 PEOPLE: When do Americans celebrate Independence Day?

4 INVENTIONS: What was the special obsession of Félix du Temple de la Croix?

5 HISTORY: What notorious road was built through the Far East to take Russian arms to China?

6 SPORT: What is the favourite pastime of a logogriphist?

7 MUSIC: Which group did Johnny Moore leave to form Johnny Moore And Slightly Adrift?

8 SCIENCE: What is measured by an anemometer?

9 THE ARTS: Who was the hero of *Wuthering Heights*?

10 FILM, TV & RADIO: Which fictitious detective employs an oriental manservant to attack him when he least expects it?

11 NATURAL HISTORY: By what, rather impolite name is the yeti sometimes known?'

12 MISCELLANY: What are the two principle ingredients of vichyssoise?

▶ **QUIZMASTER:** What do the two Greek words which combine to make 'dinosaur' mean?

TRIVIA QUIZ 124

1 MISCELLANY: How many fences are there in the Grand National?

2 GEOGRAPHY & TRAVEL: What is cultivated in the 25 kilometres of old quarry caves at Les Roches, near Paris?

3 PEOPLE: Who is the reigning monarch of Denmark?

4 INVENTIONS: What happens in the carburettor of a car?

5 HISTORY: What were macaronis in 18th century society?

6 SPORT: Which sport is played for the Air Canada Silver Broom?

7 MUSIC: Who held the number one spot in Britain for 27 weeks with 'I Believe'?

8 SCIENCE: In which century was the first medical reference to spectacles made?

9 THE ARTS: Which British sculptor drew pictures of people sleeping in tube stations during the Blitz?

10 FILM, TV & RADIO: Who played Bet Lynch's first boyfriend in 1970 and then turned up in *Brookside* 15 years later?

11 NATURAL HISTORY: What is a dragonfly called between the stages of egg and adulthood?

12 MISCELLANY: What was the motoring speed limit in Britain before 1930?

▶ **QUIZMASTER:** What type of suit, fashionable in the 40s, had a long loose jacket and high-waisted, tapering trousers?

ANSWERS 123

1 Marilyn Monroe.

2 Hong Kong.

3 July 4.

4 Aviation (he was the first man to fly 50 metres in 1890).

5 The Burma Road.

6 Crosswords.

7 The Drifters.

8 The direction and force of the wind.

9 Heathcliff.

10 Inspector Clouseau.

11 'The Abominable Snowman'.

12 Leeks and potatoes.

■ Terrible lizard.

ANSWERS 124

1 30.

2 Mushrooms.

3 Queen Margrethe II.

4 Petrol and air are mixed together.

5 Dandies.

6 Curling.

7 Frankie Laine.

8 The 14th (1303).

9 Henry Moore.

10 Tommy Boyle.

11 A nymph.

12 20 mph (though it was widely ignored).

■ The zoot suit.

1 MISCELLANY: Who is the commander in chief of the British armed forces?

2 GEOGRAPHY & TRAVEL: What covers the major part of the earth's surface, land or sea?

3 PEOPLE: If you belonged to the BAOR, where would you live?

4 INVENTIONS: What do astronauts wear to stop their blood from boiling on space walks?

5 HISTORY: In what field did Maria Montessori make her name?

6 SPORT: What race did Eddie Merckx win four times in succession?

7 MUSIC: Which former manager of The Yardbirds and Marc Bolan currently manages Wham!?

8 SCIENCE: What colour does litmus paper turn in acid solutions?

9 THE ARTS: Who eats Cow Pie?

10 FILM, TV & RADIO: Which situation comedy character staged his own suicide in the last episode?

11 NATURAL HISTORY: How many of these trees are native to Britain: Scots pine, yew, juniper?

12 MISCELLANY: Which of these countries abolished slavery first: Holland, Denmark, Chile, England, America?

▶ QUIZMASTER: To what piece of Norman office equipment does the word exchequer refer in relation to the Chancellor's office?

TRIVIA QUIZ 126

1 MISCELLANY: Who became Prime Minister in 1923?

2 GEOGRAPHY & TRAVEL: What slang word derives from 'Prisoners of Mother England'?

3 PEOPLE: How many MPs are there in the House Of Commons?

4 INVENTIONS: What is the raw material for high quality, hand-made paper?

5 HISTORY: Which famous Englishman was killed at The Battle Of Trafalgar?

6 SPORT: What did Takaaki Dan win in 1978/79?

7 MUSIC: Who is August Darnell better known as?

8 SCIENCE: What is measured by a seismograph?

9 THE ARTS: In which book lurk loathsome orcs?

10 FILM, TV & RADIO: Who was the Yorkshire-born host of *Have A Go*?

11 NATURAL HISTORY: What part of the human anatomy has 9,000 buds?

12 MISCELLANY: How many counters does each player have in backgammon?

▶ QUIZMASTER: Where would you expect a Venusian to live?

ANSWERS 125

1 The Queen.

2 Sea.

3 Germany. (The initials stand for British Army Of The Rhine.)

4 Pressurized suits.

5 Infant teaching.

6 The Tour de France.

7 Simon Napier-Bell.

8 Red.

9 Desperate Dan.

10 Reginald Perrin (in *The Fall And Rise Of Reginald Perrin*).

11 All three.

12 Chile in 1786.

■ The squared cloth on which an account of revenue was kept with counters.

ANSWERS 126

1 Stanley Baldwin.

2 Pommy, the Australian slang for English immigrants.

3 650.

4 Cotton and linen rags.

5 Horatio Nelson.

6 The World Disco Dancing Championship.

7 Kid Creole.

8 Earthquakes.

9 *The Lord Of The Rings*.

10 Wilfred Pickles.

11 The tongue.

12 15.

■ Venus.

TRIVIA QUIZ 127

1 MISCELLANY: What is the name of the mythical giant who saved himself from the flood by climbing on to the roof of Noah's Ark?

2 GEOGRAPHY & TRAVEL: What is the capital of Nova Scotia?

3 PEOPLE: Why was Mrs Janet Walton in the news in 1983?

4 INVENTIONS: What joins the crankshaft to the piston in a car engine?

5 HISTORY: Which British sovereign had the longest reign?

6 SPORT: Who was World Heavyweight Boxing Champion immediately after Joe Louis?

7 MUSIC: Who did Stephen Foster entreat not to cry for him in his famous song?

8 SCIENCE: In which human sense does the Purkinje effect manifest itself?

9 THE ARTS: Which poet died of rheumatic fever while leading the Greeks against the Turks?

10 FILM, TV & RADIO: Which woman singer appeared in *Mad Max III*?

11 NATURAL HISTORY: What is a beaver's home called?

12 MISCELLANY: What is the practical unit of electrical resistance?

▶ **QUIZMASTER:** What happens to milk when it's kept in a thermos flask for a week?

TRIVIA QUIZ 128

1 MISCELLANY: What were the dispossessed farmers from the Dust Bowl region of America during the 1930s called?

2 GEOGRAPHY & TRAVEL: What island of 840,000 square miles was ruled by Denmark until 1979?

3 PEOPLE: Which country has the largest number of doctors?

4 INVENTIONS: Who invented the modern safety razor?

5 HISTORY: How old is *The Domesday Book*?

6 SPORT: Which new water sport was added to the Olympic repertoire in 1984?

7 MUSIC: Which Spanish dance appears in Mozart's *Figaro* and is the title of a ZZ Top album?

8 SCIENCE: What physical force is the *raison d'être* of the funfair's Wall Of Death?

9 THE ARTS: Which world figure wrote a play called *The Jeweller's Shop*?

10 FILM, TV & RADIO: Which thriller writer dramatised the life of Christ for a radio serial?

11 NATURAL HISTORY: What are plants that live for one year called?

12 MISCELLANY: What pump functions 2,500 million times in 70 years?

▶ **QUIZMASTER:** Who was the first (and probably only) animated cartoon sex symbol?

ANSWERS 127

1 Og.

2 Halifax.

3 She gave birth to sextuplets.

4 The connecting rod.

5 Queen Victoria.

6 Ezzard Charles

7 Susanna.

8 Sight. (In poor illumination the eye is more sensitive to blue light.)

9 Byron.

10 Tina Turner.

11 A lodge.

12 The ohm.

■ It goes bad.

ANSWERS 128

1 Okies.

2 Greenland.

3 The USSR.

4 Gillette.

5 900 years. (It was completed in 1086.)

6 Synchronized swimming.

7 Fandango.

8 Centrifugal force.

9 Pope John Paul II.

10 Dorothy L. Sayers (*The Man Born To Be King*).

11 Annuals.

12 The human heart.

■ Betty Boop.

TRIVIA QUIZ 129

1 MISCELLANY: Where would you expect to find the colours gules, azure, pourpre, vert, sable and argent?

2 GEOGRAPHY AND TRAVEL: What is the capital of Guatemala?

3 PEOPLE: Who are Jains?

4 INVENTIONS: What is the purpose of a helicopter's tail rotor?

5 HISTORY: Where did Tyburn gallows stand in London?

6 SPORT: When did Tony Jacklin win the British Open Golf Championship?

7 MUSIC: Which sizeable star claims he revs up for his performances with four tots of tequila and a top-up from an oxygen tank?

8 SCIENCE: Which profession sought to turn base metals into gold?

9 THE ARTS: In which city is the *Book Of Kells*?

10 FILM, TV & RADIO: What was Steve McQueen's last film?

11 NATURAL HISTORY: Name two of the three main parts of an insect's body.

12 MISCELLANY: Which relative did Oedipus kill?

▶ **QUIZMASTER:** In which film did the director, as a joke, make his leading villain say, 'My mother isn't herself today'?

TRIVIA QUIZ 130

1 MISCELLANY: Who wrote a poem which begins: 'I wandered lonely as a cloud'?

2 GEOGRAPHY & TRAVEL: What is North America's longest river?

3 PEOPLE: What is another name for the Yeoman Of The Guard?

4 INVENTIONS: What is the 'calibre' of a gun?

5 HISTORY: What disaster is remembered in the children's rhyme 'Ring-a-Ring O Roses'?

6 SPORT: By what name is the Spanish-based sport jai alai better known?

7 MUSIC: Which 18th century German-born composer became a British subject?

8 SCIENCE: Which book did Charles Darwin publish in 1859?

9 THE ARTS: By what name is the painting 'La Giaconda' better known in England?

10 FILM, TV & RADIO: In which town did The Flintstones live?

11 NATURAL HISTORY: Who introduced pheasants to Britain?

12 MISCELLANY: What is considered the oldest city to have a continuing existence in the world?

▶ **QUIZMASTER:** If you were served *cuy* in Peru, what would you be eating?

ANSWERS 129

1 On coats of arms.

2 Guatemala City.

3 Followers of an Indian religious sect.

4 To stop the body spinning round with the main rotor.

5 Marble Arch.

6 1969.

7 Meat Loaf.

8 Alchemy.

9 Dublin.

10 *The Hunter* (1980).

11 Head, thorax, abdomen.

12 His father.

■ *Psycho.*

ANSWERS 130

1 William Wordsworth.

2 The Missouri.

3 Beefeaters.

4 The inside diameter of the barrel.

5 The Great Plague, also known as the Black Death.

6 Pelota.

7 Handel.

8 *The Origin Of The Species By Natural Selection.*

9 The Mona Lisa.

10 Bedrock.

11 The Romans.

12 Damascus.

■ Guinea pig.

TRIVIA QUIZ 131

1 MISCELLANY: Why is the grapefruit so named?

2 GEOGRAPHY & TRAVEL: What is the world's second largest country?

3 PEOPLE: What do the initials COHSE stand for?

4 INVENTIONS: In what city did Guglielmo Marconi first transmit a radio signal?

5 HISTORY: Who ordered the tide to retreat?

6 SPORT: What, in photography, does SLR mean?

7 MUSIC: Which 60s group was idolised by Haircut One Hundred?

8 SCIENCE: Who said of the lever: 'Give me a firm spot on which to stand and I will move the Earth'?

9 THE ARTS: What kind of people lived in Lilliput?

10 FILM, TV & RADIO: Who won a best supporting actor oscar for his role in *The Killing Fields*?

11 NATURAL HISTORY: What is the fruit of the blackthorn?

12 MISCELLANY: By which river did George Armstrong Custer make his last stand?

▶ QUIZMASTER: What was it that Miss Buss and Miss Beale could not feel?

TRIVIA QUIZ 132

1 MISCELLANY: Where in London is the sailing clipper The Cutty Sark kept?

2 GEOGRAPHY & TRAVEL: What are the two main rivers of Iraq?

3 PEOPLE: What does the bursar of a school or college look after?

4 INVENTIONS: What is half the world's production of copper used to conduct?

5 HISTORY: What was the last food category to come off rationing after World War II?

6 SPORT: How many arrows does an archer shoot in an international competition?

7 MUSIC: Who is the self-styled king of New York Hip Hop?

8 SCIENCE: Who first advanced the theory that matter is composed of indestructible atoms?

9 THE ARTS: How many years was Robinson Crusoe stranded on his island?

10 FILM, TV & RADIO: Who played the title role in *Ironside*?

11 NATURAL HISTORY: Why is the puffin sometimes called the sea parrot?

12 MISCELLANY: Who designed Regent Street, London in 1811?

▶ QUIZMASTER: What was Bugs Bunny's first recorded word?

ANSWERS 131

1 Because it grows in grape-like bunches.

2 Canada.

3 Confederation of Health Service Employees.

4 London.

5 King Canute.

6 Single lens reflex.

7 The Monkees.

8 Archimedes.

9 Very short ones.

10 Haing S. Ngor.

11 The sloe.

12 Little Big Horn.

■ Cupid's darts.

ANSWERS 132

1 Greenwich.

2 The Tigris and the Euphrates.

3 Finance.

4 Electricity.

5 Meat.

6 72.

7 Afrika Bambaataa.

8 Democritus (in the fifth century BC).

9 28.

10 Raymond Burr.

11 Because of its brightly coloured bill.

12 John Nash.

■ 'What's'.

TRIVIA QUIZ 133

1 MISCELLANY: Who is The Man With No Name?

2 GEOGRAPHY & TRAVEL: What is the nearest country to Jersey?

3 PEOPLE: Which Italian explorer discovered Newfoundland?

4 INVENTIONS: What is the connection between the cigarette and 16th century Spanish beggars?

5 HISTORY: Which two sides fought in the Six Day War?

6 SPORT: What is a Cape triangular?

7 MUSIC: How many strings has a balalaika?

8 SCIENCE: What measure of electrical motive force when applied to a conductor of one ohm resistance, produces a current of one ampere?

9 THE ARTS: Who was the Poet Laureate before John Betjeman?

10 FILM, TV & RADIO: Who wrote *Amadeus*?

11 NATURAL HISTORY: How does the goat moth get its name?

12 MISCELLANY: What did the Reverend Robert Hawker dress up as when he sat on a rock off the Cornish coast in 1825?

▶ QUIZMASTER: What word at various times has had these meanings: mistress, a bargeman, a servant, a demon and a dog?

TRIVIA QUIZ 134

1 MISCELLANY: Which monarch declared that a yard should be 36 inches?

2 GEOGRAPHY & TRAVEL: What is unusual about the location of the Jag Nivas Hotel, once the palace of an Indian prince?

3 PEOPLE: Which country has the most official immigrants?

4 INVENTIONS: What city was originally built on wooden piles driven into the mud of a lagoon?

5 HISTORY: What was found at Sutton Hoo in 1939?

6 SPORT: What is the first bridge passed in the Oxford and Cambridge Boat Race?

7 MUSIC: Who released a single celebrating the birthday of Martin Luther King?

8 SCIENCE: There are about 30 million of them in one drop of blood. What are they?

9 THE ARTS: Which planet did Superman come from?

10 FILM, TV & RADIO: Where was Liz Taylor's husband and film producer Mike Todd heading when his plane crashed into a mountain on March 22 1958?

11 NATURAL HISTORY: What is the American name for maize?

12 MISCELLANY: How many edges are there on a möbius strip?

▶ QUIZMASTER: What is the first word in the dictionary?

ANSWERS 133

1 The Clint Eastwood character established in *A Fistful Of Dollars*.

2 France.

3 John Cabot.

4 They invented it. (They picked up cigar butts and rolled the scraps in paper, calling them cigarillos.)

5 Arabs and Israelis.

6 A postage stamp.

7 Three.

8 One volt.

9 Cecil Day Lewis.

10 Peter Shaffer.

11 Because it smells like a goat.

12 A mermaid.

■ Pug.

ANSWERS 134

1 Henry I (it is said to be the length of his arm).

2 It is in the middle of a lake.

3 USA.

4 Venice.

5 An Anglo-Saxon burial ship.

6 Hammersmith Bridge.

7 Stevie Wonder.

8 Corpuscles.

9 Krypton.

10 He was travelling to an award ceremony to be named 'Showman Of The Year'.

11 Corn.

12 One.

■ A.

TRIVIA QUIZ 135

1 MISCELLANY: Which Swiss hero led a 14th century uprising against the Austrians and is celebrated in an opera?

2 GEOGRAPHY & TRAVEL: In which county is Canterbury?

3 PEOPLE: Which British woman sailed solo across the Atlantic in 1976?

4 INVENTIONS: What did Donald Bailey design in World War II?

5 HISTORY: Who said 'history is bunk'?

6 SPORT: Who was the English cricket captain during the 'bodyline' tour of 1932/33?

7 MUSIC: For what performing troupe did Stravinsky compose a special polka in 1942?

8 SCIENCE: What do you call stars that are so dense that light cannot escape from them?

9 THE ARTS: What was Uncas the last of?

10 FILM, TV & RADIO: What do Sean Connery, George Lazenby and Roger Moore have in common?

11 NATURAL HISTORY: Where did oranges originate?

12 MISCELLANY: What star wedding of 1956 inspired the headline 'Egghead weds Hourglass'?

▶ QUIZMASTER: Who travels under the aliases Knecht Ruprecht and Robin Goodfellow?

TRIVIA QUIZ 136

1 MISCELLANY: Whose 1961 hit 'Tribute To Buddy Holly' was banned by the BBC?

2 GEOGRAPHY & TRAVEL: Where did the Sun King choose to build a palace half a mile long?

3 PEOPLE: Which religious leader built up a famous racing stable?

4 INVENTIONS: Who first proposed that the thermometer be divided into 100 degrees?

5 HISTORY: Which prison was attacked at the beginning of the French Revolution?

6 SPORT: By what measure is the strength of beer calculated?

7 MUSIC: Who erased her 60s little girl image with a harsh album called *Broken English*?

8 SCIENCE: Fossils of what were found at Olduvai Gorge?

9 THE ARTS: Which children's book features Mole, Ratty and Badger?

10 FILM, TV & RADIO: Which 1938 radio play caused Americans to flee their homes in panic?

11 NATURAL HISTORY: In which of the two polar regions do penguins live?

12 MISCELLANY: Who said 'It's not the men in my life, it's the life in my men that counts'?

▶ QUIZMASTER: What name is given to an amateur sportsman who nevertheless contrives to make a lot of money?

ANSWERS 135

1 William Tell.

2 Kent.

3 Clare Francis.

4 The Bailey bridge.

5 Henry Ford.

6 Douglas Jardine.

7 The elephant troupe of the Barnum and Bailey circus (*'Circus Polka'*).

8 Black holes.

9 The Mohicans.

10 They all played James Bond.

11 China.

12 Arthur Miller and Marilyn Monroe.

■ Father Christmas.

ANSWERS 136

1 Mike Berry's.

2 Versailles.

3 Aga Khan III.

4 Celsius.

5 The Bastille.

6 Specific gravity.

7 Marianne Faithfull.

8 Early man.

9 *The Wind In The Willows*.

10 Orson Welles' production of H.G. Wells' *War Of The Worlds*.

11 The Antarctic.

12 Mae West.

■ A shamateur.

TRIVIA QUIZ 137

1 MISCELLANY: Who was the first Tsar?

2 GEOGRAPHY & TRAVEL: What leaves Tokyo every 15-20 minutes at speeds of up to 156 mph?

3 PEOPLE: Who lived at 10 Rillington Place?

4 INVENTIONS: Name one of the differences that makes red phosphorus more appropriate than white phosphorus in the manufacture of safety matches.

5 HISTORY: Which country did Brian Boru rule?

6 SPORT: What do Australian cricketers call extras?

7 MUSIC: Which 70s star was forced by bankruptcy to sell his shimmering costumes to fans?

8 SCIENCE: We don't normally have to carry it around with us, but a large jet airliner might use 35 tons of it on an Atlantic crossing. What is it?

9 THE ARTS: In the Arthurian legends, what is the name of King Arthur's queen?

10 FILM, TV & RADIO: Which 1921 silent film was recently re-released with a disco soundtrack?

11 NATURAL HISTORY: Who introduced potatoes to Britain?

12 MISCELLANY: What is the church of the Mormons called?

▶ QUIZMASTER: Which illegal practice in racing is named after a horse called Hobbie Noble?

TRIVIA QUIZ 138

1 MISCELLANY: What drug, used to relieve pain, is obtained from the opium poppy?

2 GEOGRAPHY & TRAVEL: What is the largest city in Africa?

3 PEOPLE: Which two British spies defected in 1951?

4 INVENTIONS: Why does the Post Office print rows of dots on post-coded letters?

5 HISTORY: What nationality was Copernicus?

6 SPORT: Which playwright named a whole cast after famous cricketers?

7 MUSIC: Which small, egg-shaped, earthenware wind instrument is nicknamed the 'sweet potato'?

8 SCIENCE: What does BASIC stand for?

9 THE ARTS: Name two of Enid Blyton's Famous Five.

10 FILM, TV & RADIO: How many programmes, to the nearest 20, does the BBC transmit daily on Radios One, Two, Three and Four?

11 NATURAL HISTORY: What do we call plants that live for several years?

12 MISCELLANY: What's the world's chief agricultural crop?

▶ QUIZMASTER: A pack of washing powder costing £3.20 is twice the height, width and breadth of another. How much, proportionately, should the smaller one cost?

ANSWERS 137

1 Ivan The Terrible.

2 The Shinkansen, or bullet trains.

3 Murderer John Reginald Christie.

4 It isn't poisonous and it doesn't ignite on contact with air.

5 Ireland.

6 Sundries.

7 Gary Glitter.

8 Oxygen.

9 Guinevere.

10 *Metropolis*.

11 Sir Walter Raleigh (from North America).

12 The Church Of Jesus Christ Of Latter-Day Saints.

■ Nobbling (Hobbie Noble was drugged).

ANSWERS 138

1 Morphine.

2 Cairo.

3 Burgess and MacLean.

4 So that they can be sorted by machine (the dots denote district and street).

5 Polish.

6 Harold Pinter.

7 The ocarina.

8 Beginner's All-purpose Symbolic Instruction Code.

9 Dick, Julian, Georgina, Anne and Timmy, the dog.

10 Between 87 and 90.

11 Perennials.

12 Cereal.

■ 40 pence.

TRIVIA QUIZ 139

1 MISCELLANY: Who said 'I myself consider myself to be the most important figure in the world'?

2 GEOGRAPHY & TRAVEL: What is Constantinople now called?

3 PEOPLE: What was Al Capone charged with in 1931?

4 INVENTIONS: John Logie Baird began studying the possibility of 'seeing by wireless' in 1906. What was the result?

5 HISTORY: Which queen supported her sons in rebellion against Henry II?

6 SPORT: What cricketing event first took place in 1963?

7 MUSIC: Who tuned his instrument down an octave and invented the 'twanging guitar'?

8 SCIENCE: What acid is found in vinegar?

9 THE ARTS: Which Spanish town, bombed during the Civil War, inspired a Picasso masterpiece?

10 FILM, TV & RADIO: Which silent film star insured his crossed eyes against uncrossing for $25,000?

11 NATURAL HISTORY: Which British mammal can grip with its tail?

12 MISCELLANY: Where was the phrase 'the spectre of communism' first coined?

▶ QUIZMASTER: Which English ruler banned mince pies in the 17th century?

TRIVIA QUIZ 140

1 MISCELLANY: Which American movie star had the Christian names William Claude?

2 GEOGRAPHY & TRAVEL: What is the name of the island on which The Empire State Building stands?

3 PEOPLE: Who was the leader of the Labour Party before Harold Wilson?

4 INVENTIONS: What eventually happens to air if it is compressed?

5 HISTORY: What was Barnum and Bailey's 'Greatest Show On Earth'?

6 SPORT: What happened for the first time in FA Cup history in the 1970 final?

7 MUSIC: What is the name for a harmonious combination of notes played simultaneously?

8 SCIENCE: Where was Archimedes when he shouted 'Eureka!'?

9 THE ARTS: Which British cathedral was consecrated in 1963?

10 FILM, TV & RADIO: Which actress cradle-snatched Benjamin in *The Graduate*?

11 NATURAL HISTORY: Which flower, the subject of a craze in the 16th century, is named after the Turkish word for turban?

12 MISCELLANY: From which country does Mother Teresa originate?

▶ QUIZMASTER: What is a zucchino?

ANSWERS 139

1 Idi Amin.

2 Istanbul.

3 Income tax evasion.

4 The television.

5 Eleanor of Aquitaine.

6 The Gillette Cup.

7 Duane Eddy.

8 Acetic acid.

9 Guernica.

10 Ben Turpin.

11 The harvest mouse.

12 The Communist Manifesto.

■ Oliver Cromwell.

ANSWERS 140

1 W.C. Fields.

2 Manhattan.

3 Hugh Gaitskell.

4 It becomes a liquid.

5 A circus.

6 It went to a replay.

7 A chord.

8 In the bath.

9 Coventry Cathedral.

10 Anne Bancroft.

11 The tulip.

12 Yugoslavia.

■ A courgette.

TRIVIA QUIZ 141

1 MISCELLANY: Which future world leader was once expelled from the Tiflis Theological Seminary for reading Karl Marx, Victor Hugo and Charles Darwin?

2 GEOGRAPHY & TRAVEL: What is the world's largest office building?

3 PEOPLE: What is Prince Charles' full name?

4 INVENTIONS: Many modern clothes are fitted with an 1891 invention. What is it?

5 HISTORY: Where did the Boxer Rebellion take place?

6 SPORT: What is the correct name for the hop, skip and jump?

7 MUSIC: Which first performance of a Handel suite was seen by more people than could hear it?

8 SCIENCE: How many fluid ounces are there in a pint?

9 THE ARTS: Which English painter made his name with 'The Boyhood of Raleigh'?

10 FILM, TV & RADIO: Who was the girl in Peter Sellers' soup in 1970?

11 NATURAL HISTORY: What are stinkhorns?

12 MISCELLANY: What are policemen up to when they practice dactyloscopy?

▶ **QUIZMASTER:** What shape would you expect a securiform object to be?

TRIVIA QUIZ 142

1 MISCELLANY: Who was the twin brother of Remus?

2 GEOGRAPHY & TRAVEL: What is the name of the fracture in the earth's crust that makes Californians nervous?

3 PEOPLE: Which two countries have St Andrew as their patron saint?

4 INVENTIONS: What is it that aircrafts' instrument landing systems 'lock on' to?

5 HISTORY: What did Scottish-born Allan Pinkerton set up in America?

6 SPORT: Name one of the three kinds of sword used in fencing.

7 MUSIC: Which group had a 1966 hit with 'Friday On My Mind'?

8 SCIENCE: Which weighs most – a ton or a tonne?

9 THE ARTS: In which Shakespearean play do the Gobbos appear?

10 FILM, TV & RADIO: In which TV police series did Ed Byrnes play a character called Kookie?

11 NATURAL HISTORY: What creature's spawn takes the form of two parallel strings of jelly several feet long?

12 MISCELLANY: Which Francis Ford Coppola film is in black and white except for a coloured fish?

▶ **QUIZMASTER:** What is the special quality of telegenic people?

ANSWERS 141

1 Joseph Stalin.

2 The World Trade Center or the Pentagon (depending how you define it).

3 Charles Philip Arthur George.

4 The zip (invented by Whitcomb L. Hudson).

5 China.

6 The Triple Jump.

7 *The Music For The Royal Fireworks*.

8 20.

9 Millais.

10 Goldie Hawn.

11 Fungi.

12 Fingerprinting.

■ Arc-shaped.

ANSWERS 142

1 Romulus.

2 The San Andreas fault.

3 Scotland and Russia.

4 Two radio positioning beams transmitted from the airfield.

5 A detective agency.

6 Epée, sabre and foil.

7 The Easybeats.

8 The ton. (One tonne is 1,000 kilogrammes and 0.984207 of a ton).

9 *The Merchant of Venice*.

10 *77 Sunset Strip*.

11 The toad's.

12 *Rumblefish*.

■ They look good on TV.

TRIVIA QUIZ 143

1 **MISCELLANY:** What kind of medicine did Nicholas Culpeper practice?

2 **GEOGRAPHY & TRAVEL:** What is the name of the enormous dam on the Nile that was completed in 1970?

3 **PEOPLE:** What does a genealogist do?

4 **INVENTIONS:** What is a cross-cut saw specifically designed to do?

5 **HISTORY:** What did William Wilberforce campaign for?

6 **SPORT:** What did Mick The Miller win twice?

7 **MUSIC:** Which former Steely Dan member released an album called *The Nightfly* in 1984?

8 **SCIENCE:** Why does baking powder cause dough to rise?

9 **THE ARTS:** Which French artist painted a landscape of South London's Penge Station?

10 **FILM, TV & RADIO:** In which city was the series *Gunsmoke* set?

11 **NATURAL HISTORY:** Seeing one is supposed to presage sorrow, but two will bring joy. What are they?

12 **MISCELLANY:** Where is Nelson buried?

▶ **QUIZMASTER:** What age was jockey J. Forth when he became the oldest Derby winner in 1829?

TRIVIA QUIZ 144

1 **MISCELLANY:** Which multi-millionaire shopkeeper's Christian names were Frank Winfield?

2 **GEOGRAPHY & TRAVEL:** Which is the only European country whose population has decreased in the last 125 years?

3 **PEOPLE:** Which writer was the mother of Shirley Williams?

4 **INVENTIONS:** Out of what kind of pipe did Galileo construct his first telescope?

5 **HISTORY:** What airport did Israeli commandos storm in a rescue mission?

6 **SPORT:** What is France's premier racing circuit?

7 **MUSIC:** Which Beatles' album had a picture of Bob Dylan on the cover?

8 **SCIENCE:** With which astronomical relationship does the metonic cycle concern itself?

9 **THE ARTS:** To which literary family do Jolyon, Jolly, Soames, Fleur and Winifred belong?

10 **FILM, TV AND RADIO:** Which actress first came to the attention of the English-speaking world in a 1923 film called *The Saga Of Gösta Berling*?

11 **NATURAL HISTORY:** The following are variations of which species: dog, tiger, hammerhead?

12 **MISCELLANY:** What holy book's title, when translated means 'That should be read'?

▶ **QUIZMASTER:** What is the name of the regular feature on the last page of the *Sunday Times* Magazine?

ANSWERS 143

1 Herbal medicine.

2 The Aswan Dam.

3 Traces family trees.

4 Cut across the grain of the wood.

5 The abolition of slavery.

6 The Greyhound Derby.

7 Donald Fagan.

8 It produces bubbles of carbon dioxide gas.

9 Pissarro.

10 Dodge City.

11 Magpies.

12 St Paul's Cathedral.

■ 60.

ANSWERS 144

1 Woolworth.

2 Ireland.

3 Vera Brittain.

4 An organ pipe.

5 Entebbe.

6 The Prix de l'Arc de Triomphe.

7 *Sergeant Peppers' Lonely Hearts Club Band.*

8 The relationship of the sun and the moon.

9 The Forsytes

10 Greta Garbo.

11 The shark.

12 *The Koran.*

■ A Life In The Day.

TRIVIA QUIZ 145

1 MISCELLANY: In which radio programme would you expect to hear the following words: Rockall, Bailey, Malin, Finisterre?

2 GEOGRAPHY & TRAVEL: Which eight-storey, white marble, Romanesque bell tower moves a quarter of an inch a year?

3 PEOPLE: Who is the current Poet Laureate?

4 INVENTIONS: What were the 1922 writtle tests by P.P. Eckersley?

5 HISTORY: Who were the original Thugs?

6 SPORT: What has 16 feathers and weighs ⅕ of an ounce?

7 MUSIC: What brought Eric Clapton, Paul McCartney, Stephen Stills, Keith Richards and PP Arnold to St Tropez Town Hall on May 12, 1971?

8 SCIENCE: What do Messier numbers refer to?

9 THE ARTS: Which Sherlock Holmes character marries Mary Morstan?

10 FILM, TV & RADIO: Actress Françoise Dorléac was killed in a car accident in 1967. Who is her actress sister?

11 NATURAL HISTORY: What is the most common bird in England and Wales?

12 MISCELLANY: For which game did the Duke of Beaufort lay down a set of rules in 1877?

QUIZMASTER: Where was Muhammad Ali sitting when he said 'Rustie, you're the greatest!'?

TRIVIA QUIZ 146

1 MISCELLANY: Who coined the phrase 'the unacceptable face of capitalism'?

2 GEOGRAPHY & TRAVEL: Where does the 'Mona Lisa' hang?

3 PEOPLE: What did Alcock and Brown achieve in 1919?

4 INVENTIONS: The Pharos of Alexandria, built in 280 BC, was the first one. What was it?

5 HISTORY: Who or what was 'Stonewall' Jackson?

6 SPORT: What was Evonne Cawley's maiden name?

7 MUSIC: What note is sounded by a tuning fork vibrating 256 times a second?

8 SCIENCE: What is sodium chloride?

9 THE ARTS: By what name was the schoolmaster Chipping better known?

10 FILM, TV & RADIO: What TV series took place in the 4077th Mobile Army Surgical Hospital?

11 NATURAL HISTORY: What is the largest reptile?

12 MISCELLANY: Which film star's statue stands in Leicester Square?

QUIZMASTER: Which American actor was awarded America's highest tribute, The Congressional Medal Of Honour?

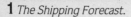

ANSWERS 145

1 *The Shipping Forecast.*

2 The Leaning Tower Of Pisa.

3 Ted Hughes.

4 The first regular broadcasts by the BBC.

5 A murderous religious sect of India.

6 A shuttlecock.

7 Mick Jagger's wedding to Bianca Perez Morena de Macias.

8 Stars. (Messier numbers are given to star clusters and nebulae.)

9 Dr Watson.

10 Catherine Deneuve.

11 The wren.

12 Badminton.

■ Rustie Lee's restaurant.

ANSWERS 146

1 Edward Heath.

2 The Louvre in Paris.

3 The first non-stop flight across the Atlantic.

4 A lighthouse.

5 An American Confederate general.

6 Goolagong.

7 Middle C.

8 Salt.

9 Mr Chips.

10 *M.A.S.H.*

11 The crocodile.

12 Charlie Chaplin's.

■ John Wayne.

TRIVIA QUIZ 147

1 MISCELLANY: What fungus is a very important ingredient of bread?

2 GEOGRAPHY & TRAVEL: Which American tourist attraction was designed by Frederic Bartholdi?

3 PEOPLE: Who wrote his thoughts in a Little Red Book?

4 INVENTIONS: What is macadam?

5 HISTORY: Who conquered an empire of nearly 5 million square miles, which stretched from the Pacific to the Caspian Sea?

6 SPORT: Name two of the five activities in the modern pentathlon.

7 MUSIC: What happens to the members of the multi-million dollar Spanish language pop group Menudo when they reach the age of 16?

8 SCIENCE: What is the name for rocks that have been molten?

9 THE ARTS: In *A Christmas Carol* who was Tiny Tim's father?

10 FILM, TV & RADIO: Which Manchurian was described by John Boulting as 'the last of the romantic actors'?

11 NATURAL HISTORY: What are swallow tails, orange tips and morphos?

12 MISCELLANY: Why does the moon shine?

▶ **QUIZMASTER:** Which disc jockey condemned Frankie Goes To Hollywood's 'Relax' on his show, thus making it a guaranteed hit?

TRIVIA QUIZ 148

1 MISCELLANY: What did Edmund Halley observe in 1682?

2 GEOGRAPHY & TRAVEL: What kind of grape is grown near Malaga, Southern Spain?

3 PEOPLE: Which government employees take the title of 'Excellency'?

4 INVENTIONS: What did Captain Charles E. Yeager achieve on October 14, 1947?

5 HISTORY: What surfaced dramatically on October 11, 1982?

6 SPORT: What is the highest-growing English flower?

7 MUSIC: Who wrote a ballet called *Whipped Cream*?

8 SCIENCE: What are 746 watts equivalent to in terms of horsepower?

9 THE ARTS: What was the name of Thomas Hardy's Mayor Of Casterbridge?

10 FILM, TV & RADIO: What did Samantha do in *Bewitched* to summon up her magic powers?

11 NATURAL HISTORY: What is a male swan called?

12 MISCELLANY: What was the first full-length animated feature film?

▶ **QUIZMASTER:** Who monkeyed about with Fay Wray?

ANSWERS 147

1 Yeast.

2 The Statue Of Liberty.

3 Chairman Mao.

4 A road surfacing material consisting of tiny chips of gravel pressed together.

5 Genghis Khan.

6 Cross-country riding, fencing, shooting, swimming and cross-country running.

7 They are dismissed and replaced (it's a condition of their contracts).

8 Igneous rocks.

9 Bob Cratchit.

10 Robert Donat.

11 Butterflies.

12 Because it reflects the sun.

■ Mike Read.

ANSWERS 148

1 Halley's comet.

2 The muscatel grape.

3 Ambassadors.

4 He was the first man to travel faster than the speed of sound.

5 The *Mary Rose*.

6 The sunflower.

7 Richard Strauss (*Schlagobers*).

8 One unit of horsepower.

9 Michael Henchard.

10 She twitched her nose.

11 A cob.

12 *Snow White*.

■ King Kong.

TRIVIA QUIZ 149

1 MISCELLANY: Who killed Orion?

2 GEOGRAPHY & TRAVEL: What language was first introduced to the world in the 1887 book *Internacia Lingyo*?

3 PEOPLE: Which country's parliament is called Storthing?

4 INVENTIONS: In a light bulb, what prevents the filament from burning up immediately?

5 HISTORY: Who was Britain's first socialist MP in 1892?

6 SPORT: In which odd sport requiring rubber footwear was a new world record of 173 feet set in 1978?

7 MUSIC: Which star received presidential permission to be buried at sea on December 28 1983?

8 SCIENCE: 'The Italian navigator has reached the New World' was a message in code sent in 1942. What did it convey?

9 THE ARTS: Who wrote the *Thomas the Tank Engine* stories?

10 FILM, TV & RADIO: Name one of the actors who played the two star athletes in *Chariots Of Fire*.

11 NATURAL HISTORY: How many hearts has a cuttlefish?

12 MISCELLANY: Why couldn't Midas eat his dinner?

▶ QUIZMASTER: What comic character made his first appearance in the 1913 film, *Kid Auto Races At Venice?*

TRIVIA QUIZ 150

1 MISCELLANY: Where did Noah's Ark land?

2 GEOGRAPHY & TRAVEL: How many times a day must a Mohammedan pray?

3 PEOPLE: What was the name of the Duchess of Windsor before she married the Duke?

4 INVENTIONS: What did veterinary surgeon John Boyd Dunlop invent in 1888?

5 HISTORY: What battle did Henry V win in 1415?

6 SPORT: With which sport do you associate the following phrases: snatch, clean and jerk?

7 MUSIC: Which ballet uses music by Chopin?

8 SCIENCE: Why did Benjamin Franklin fly a kite?

9 THE ARTS: Who created *The Kraken*?

10 FILM, TV & RADIO: Which James Bond theme was written by Paul McCartney?

11 NATURAL HISTORY: How do an owls' feet differ from the feet of the other birds' of prey?

12 MISCELLANY: Who played Marshall Matt Dillon in the TV series *Gunsmoke*?

▶ QUIZMASTER: What did the bells of St Martin say?

ANSWERS 149

1 Artemis.

2 Esperanto.

3 Norway's.

4 The fact that it is starved of oxygen because the glass seals it in a vacuum.

5 James Keir Hardy.

6 Welly hurling.

7 Beach Boy Dennis Wilson.

8 The fact that atomic energy had been successfully produced. (It was sent by Italian physicist Enrico Fermi.)

9 The Reverend W. Audry.

10 Ben Cross and Nigel Havers.

11 Three.

12 Because it turned to gold when he touched it.

■ Charlie Chaplin's tramp figure.

ANSWERS 150

1 Mount Ararat.

2 Five.

3 Wallis Simpson.

4 The pneumatic tyre (air-filled tyre).

5 Agincourt.

6 Weight lifting.

7 *Les Sylphides*.

8 To prove that lightning is associated with electricity.

9 John Wyndham.

10 *Live And Let Die*.

11 They are covered with feathers.

12 James Arness.

■ 'I owe you five farthings'.

TRIVIA QUIZ 151

1 MISCELLANY: Which British industrial organisation has the largest annual turnover?

2 GEOGRAPHY & TRAVEL: Which capital city begins and ends with the letter 'o'?

3 PEOPLE: Where would a Muscovite come from?

4 INVENTIONS: What did Samuel Colt invent in 1836?

5 HISTORY: Which island was recaptured first by the British in the Falklands War?

6 SPORT: Which two brothers played in England's World Cup winning soccer team in 1966?

7 MUSIC: Whose video showed nothing but a succession of faces fading into each other?

8 SCIENCE: What metal is extracted from galena?

9 THE ARTS: Which Grace Metallious book became a film and an early soap opera?

10 FILM, TV & RADIO: What do Net Als Toen and Abba have in common?

11 NATURAL HISTORY: Birds have no teeth. How do they 'chew' their food?

12 MISCELLANY: Who gave more than 1,000 performances in the stage version of the musical *Hello Dolly*?

▶ QUIZMASTER: What do the following films have in common: *Freebie And The Bean*, *The Life And Times Of Judge Roy Bean* and *Jack And The Beanstalk*?

TRIVIA QUIZ 152

1 MISCELLANY: In which TV series did the character Jamie Sommers appear?

2 GEOGRAPHY & TRAVEL: In which sea are the shipping areas Viking, Cromarty, Dogger and German Bight?

3 PEOPLE: Whose motto is 'ich dien'?

4 INVENTIONS: Who first predicted that a large amount of energy could be produced by destroying a small mass?

5 HISTORY: What did Robert Clive found in the 18th century?

6 SPORT: Omar Sharif was a player of international class at which competitive games?

7 MUSIC: What is the sub-title of Gilbert and Sullivan's *The Mikado*?

8 SCIENCE: Which did man use first, iron or bronze?

9 THE ARTS: Which English musical featured a song called 'The Student Ponce'?

10 FILM, TV & RADIO: What is the surname of millionaire detectives Jonathan and Jennifer?

11 NATURAL HISTORY: What is the main habitat of an arboreal animal?

12 MISCELLANY: What proportion of an eight carat gold ring is pure gold?

▶ QUIZMASTER: Four notes were used as a time signal by BBC radio during the war. What do they more usually herald?

ANSWERS 151

1 British Petroleum (£34,584 million in 1982).

2 Oslo.

3 Moscow.

4 The revolver.

5 South Georgia.

6 Bobby and Jackie Charlton.

7 Godley and Creme's 'Cry'.

8 Lead.

9 *Peyton Place.*

10 They were both Eurovision Song Contest winners (Net Als Toen were Dutch).

11 They swallow grit to grind the food in their stomach.

12 Carol Channing.

■ They all have Bean in the title.

ANSWERS 152

1 *The Bionic Woman*

2 The North Sea.

3 The Prince Of Wales.

4 Albert Einstein.

5 British India.

6 Bridge and Backgammon.

7 *The Town Of Titipu.*

8 Bronze.

9 *Fings Ain't What They Used To Be.*

10 Hart (in the TV series *Hart to Hart*).

11 Trees.

12 One third.

■ Beethoven's Fifth Symphony. (The rhythm is morse code for V.)

TRIVIA QUIZ 153

1 MISCELLANY: What colour is chlorophyll?

2 GEOGRAPHY & TRAVEL: What is the population density per square mile of London (to the nearest thousand)?

3 PEOPLE: In which country was Adolf Eichmann hanged for war crimes?

4 INVENTIONS: What indigestible confectionary is made from the juice of the sapodilla tree?

5 HISTORY: What did the Luddites do in the 19th century?

6 SPORT: From which country is the football club Benfica?

7 MUSIC: What is the name of the American 24-hour rock video channel?

8 SCIENCE: In what rock is aluminium found?

9 THE ARTS: Which writer lived at the Villa Mauresque?

10 FILM, TV & RADIO: What was the name of Hopalong Cassidy's horse?

11 NATURAL HISTORY: Which animal is sometimes said to be 'in velvet'?

12 MISCELLANY: What are the four basic operations of mathematics?

► QUIZMASTER: Which two countries were Britain's allies in World War I and its enemies in World War II?

TRIVIA QUIZ 154

1 MISCELLANY: What insulating material comes courtesy of the eider duck?

2 GEOGRAPHY & TRAVEL: What is England's southernmost point?

3 PEOPLE: What organisation did the Reverend Chad Varah found?

4 INVENTIONS: In which country was whisky invented?

5 HISTORY: Why did beacons blaze on English hills in 1588?

6 SPORT: What was Billie-Jean King's maiden name?

7 MUSIC: Which keyboard instrument, formerly known as a hydraulis, dates from the third century BC?

8 SCIENCE: Which planet takes 249 years to orbit the sun?

9 THE ARTS: In which book is Ford Prefect the hero?

10 FILM, TV & RADIO: Which character entered *Dynasty* dramatically by walking into La Mirage and demanding 'a bedroom for my wardrobe and one for myself'?

11 NATURAL HISTORY: What is a female rabbit called?

12 MISCELLANY: What poisonous gas is present in motor car exhaust?

► QUIZMASTER: The Persian phrase 'shah mat' appears in a corrupted form in which popular board game?

ANSWERS 153

1 Green.

2 4,238.

3 Israel.

4 Chewing gum.

5 Smashed newly introduced factory machinery.

6 Portugal.

7 MTV.

8 Bauxite.

9 Somerset Maugham.

10 Topper.

11 The deer (when its antlers are growing).

12 Addition, subtraction, multiplication and division.

■ Italy and Japan.

ANSWERS 154

1 Eider down.

2 The Lizard, Cornwall.

3 The Samaritans.

4 Ireland.

5 The Spanish Armada was sighted.

6 Moffett.

7 The organ.

8 Pluto.

9 *A Hitch Hiker's Guide To The Galaxy*.

10 Dominique.

11 A doe.

12 Carbon monoxide.

■ Chess (check mate is the form used now, the Persian expression means 'the king is dead').

TRIVIA QUIZ 155 ▶

1 **MISCELLANY:** How many dessert spoonfuls equal one table spoonful?

2 **GEOGRAPHY & TRAVEL:** The longest continuous railway track in the world (5,778 miles) starts at Moscow. Where does it end?

3 **PEOPLE:** Who was the first prime minister of Malawi?

4 **INVENTIONS:** How was chlorine used in World War I?

5 **HISTORY:** Where was Britain's first stretch of motorway opened in 1958?

6 **SPORT:** Which county won cricket's Gillette Cup the first two years?

7 **MUSIC:** Who had a number one US hit in 1982 with a little help from his friend Jennifer Warnes?

8 **SCIENCE:** The hydrogen atom contains one electron and one proton. Which carries a negative charge?

9 **THE ARTS:** What is Blofeld's Christian name in the Bond novels?

10 **FILM, TV & RADIO:** Which film star took a year out of her career to work for UNICEF?

11 **NATURAL HISTORY:** What animal lives in a citadel?

12 **MISCELLANY:** To which family of tree does the cedar belong?

▶ **QUIZMASTER:** How many years in a millennium?

TRIVIA QUIZ 156 ▶

1 How many sheets of paper in a quire?

2 **GEOGRAPHY & TRAVEL:** Which British city started life as a minor fort at the eastern end of Hadrian's Wall?

3 **PEOPLE:** What do Americans call a roundabout?

4 **INVENTIONS:** Who invented the phonograph and the electric light bulb?

5 **HISTORY:** What is the world's oldest army?

6 **SPORT:** Which sport was revitalised by the coming of colour TV?

7 **MUSIC:** In which type of band is the pan the principal instrument?

8 **SCIENCE:** What is the metric equivalent of 2.2 lbs?

9 **THE ARTS:** What is the second book in the *Lord Of The Rings* trilogy?

10 **FILM, TV & RADIO:** By what collective title are Neil, Rick, Mike and Vivyan better known?

11 **NATURAL HISTORY:** What are the following: emperor, garden tiger, death's head hawk?

12 **MISCELLANY:** How is Richard Starkey better known?

▶ **QUIZMASTER:** Which emperor had his horse elected a consul of Rome?

ANSWERS 155

1 Two.

2 Siberia.

3 Dr Hastings Banda.

4 As a poison gas.

5 Bypassing Preston (now part of the M6).

6 Sussex.

7 Joe Cocker.

8 The electron.

9 Ernst.

10 Liv Ullman.

11 The mole.

12 Pine.

■ 1,000.

ANSWERS 156

1 24.

2 Newcastle-upon-Tyne.

3 A traffic circle.

4 Thomas Eddison.

5 The Vatican City's Swiss Guard.

6 Snooker.

7 The steel band.

8 One kilogramme.

9 *The Two Towers*.

10 *The Young Ones*.

11 Moths.

12 Ringo Starr.

■ Caligula.

TRIVIA QUIZ 157

1 MISCELLANY: What is the name of the starship captained by James T. Kirk?

2 GEOGRAPHY & TRAVEL: In 1985 which two countries reached agreement on joining the EEC?

3 PEOPLE: What do misogynists dislike?

4 INVENTIONS: Which British scientist designed the R100 airship, the Wellington bomber and the bouncing bomb?

5 HISTORY: What happened to the High Priest's servant Malchus, when Jesus was arrested?

6 SPORT: How long is the Derby course?

7 MUSIC: Which annual rock fesitval uses a 50 foot high pyramidal stage that doubles as a cow shed the rest of the year?

8 SCIENCE: What is the American word for aluminium?

9 THE ARTS: At which London gallery was there a major Renoir exhibition in 1985?

10 FILM, TV & RADIO: Fred Astaire's sister was his early dance partner. What was her name?

11 NATURAL HISTORY: Why does a snake charmer jerk his pipe and sway while he is playing?

12 MISCELLANY: What is the correct name for a person who practises yoga?

▶ QUIZMASTER: What is a number system with a base of two known as?

TRIVIA QUIZ 158

1 MISCELLANY: What colour do you get if you mix green and red light?

2 GEOGRAPHY & TRAVEL: What is the Iron Curtain?

3 PEOPLE: What is a Lama?

4 INVENTIONS: What is ethylene glycol used for in cars?

5 HISTORY: Which Dorset 'martyrs' were transported for taking an illegal oath?

6 SPORT: What do the initials MCC stand for?

7 MUSIC: Who released a double album, each side exactly 16.1 minutes long, of unrelenting noise, called *Metal Machine Music* (1975)?

8 SCIENCE: What percentage of the total mass of the solar system is taken up by the sun, to the nearest one percent?

9 THE ARTS: Name one of the Shakespearean characters who goes to live in a cave.

10 FILM, TV & RADIO: Which animal was the bane of Officer Dibble's life?

11 NATURAL HISTORY: What can be found in the following varieties: spider, giant, sponge?

12 MISCELLANY: What were dachshunds bred to hunt in Germany?

▶ QUIZMASTER: What lies 16 feet beneath the North Pole?

1 USS Enterprise.

2 Spain and Portugal.

3 Women.

4 Barnes Wallis.

5 His ear was cut off.

6 One and a half miles.

7 Glastonbury.

8 Aluminum (they drop the final i).

9 The Hayward Gallery.

10 Adèle Astaire.

11 Because snakes are deaf; they are affected by the movement.

12 A yogi.

■ Binary.

ANSWERS 158

1 Yellow.

2 The border between Europe and the Warsaw Pact countries.

3 A Tibetan priest.

4 Antifreeze.

5 The Tolpuddle Martyrs.

6 Marylebone Cricket Club.

7 Lou Reed.

8 99.87.

9 Prospero or Timon of Athens.

10 Top Cat.

11 Crabs.

12 Badgers.

■ Sea (The Arctic Ocean).

TRIVIA QUIZ 159 ▶

1 MISCELLANY: What does a barometer measure?

2 GEOGRAPHY & TRAVEL: Which London station was said to look more like a cathedral on completion in 1868?

3 PEOPLE: Which country was formerly called Tanganyika?

4 INVENTIONS: What took place at Alamogordo, New Mexico in July 1945?

5 HISTORY: Who said that the Battle Of Waterloo was won on the playing fields of Eton?

6 SPORT: In which game is a ball struck against a wall with a gloved hand?

7 MUSIC: How many husbands has Tammy 'Stand By Your Man' Wynette had?

8 SCIENCE: What drug was obtained from the bark of the cinchona?

9 THE ARTS: Name three of Dorothy's companions in *The Wizard Of Oz*?

10 FILM, TV & RADIO: What was the other nickname of The Caped Crusader?

11 NATURAL HISTORY: What plant has hands and fingers?

12 MISCELLANY: What was the kingdom of Canute?

▶ **QUIZMASTER:** What is most people's most handed-down possession?

TRIVIA QUIZ 160 ▶

1 MISCELLANY: What do camels store in their humps to sustain them in the desert?

2 GEOGRAPHY & TRAVEL: Who built the Menai Suspension Bridge?

3 PEOPLE: What is the official country residence of the British prime minister?

4 INVENTIONS: Since 1967, what standard has been set by the frequency of an atomic beam of the element cesium-133?

5 HISTORY: What famous event happened in Boston harbour?

6 SPORT: What was Captain Webb the first to do?

7 MUSIC: Who wrote 'If I Were A Carpenter'?

8 SCIENCE: What was streptomycin first used to combat in 1946?

9 THE ARTS: Which English writer was born Josef Korzeniowski?

10 FILM, TV & RADIO: Not only did the top ten group The Archies not play their own instruments, but they weren't real people. What were they?

11 NATURAL HISTORY: How do lizards differ from other reptiles?

12 MISCELLANY: What are Andromeda and The Milky Way?

▶ **QUIZMASTER:** Which empire did the Spaniard Cortes conquer with 508 soldiers, 108 sailors and 16 horses?

ANSWERS 159

1 Atmospheric pressure.

2 St Pancras.

3 Tanzania.

4 The first atomic explosion.

5 The Duke Of Wellington.

6 Fives.

7 Five.

8 Quinine.

9 The Scarecrow, The Tin Man, the Cowardly Lion and Toto the dog.

10 Batman.

11 The banana. A bunch of bananas is called a hand and each banana is called a finger.

12 England.

■ Money.

ANSWERS 160

1 Fat.

2 Thomas Telford.

3 Chequers.

4 The standard measure of time.

5 The Boston Tea Party.

6 Swim the English Channel.

7 Tim Hardin.

8 Tuberculosis.

9 Joseph Conrad.

10 TV cartoon characters.

11 They don't lay eggs.

12 Galaxies.

■ The Aztec Empire.

TRIVIA QUIZ 161

1 MISCELLANY: What is the correct name for the treatment of disease by means of chemicals?

2 GEOGRAPHY & TRAVEL: What word means 'sail round'?

3 PEOPLE: What did Gottlieb Daimler patent in 1885?

4 INVENTIONS: What was the achievement of the sheep, hen and duck associates of the Montgolfier Brothers early in 1783?

5 HISTORY: Who made Christianity the official religion of the Roman Empire?

6 SPORT: Who was the first Pakistani batsman to make 100 centuries?

7 MUSIC: What was the first song sung by Stevie Wonder to reach number one in Britain?

8 SCIENCE: Why do you see the lightning flash before you hear the thunderclap?

9 THE ARTS: In which prison was Little Dorrit's father incarcerated?

10 FILM, TV & RADIO: Who said 'Beaulah, peel me a grape'?

11 NATURAL HISTORY: How many legs does an insect have?

12 MISCELLANY: What are astronauts called in the Soviet Union?

▶ QUIZMASTER: What, though once forbidden, is now the world's favourite fruit?

TRIVIA QUIZ 162

1 MISCELLANY: How many dozen in a gross?

2 GEOGRAPHY & TRAVEL: Which American state was the first to discover oil?

3 PEOPLE: What does Reuters collect?

4 INVENTIONS: What was the first important means of industrial transport in Britain?

5 HISTORY: What world crisis occurred in 1956?

6 SPORT: Who was Tottenham Hotspur's goalkeeper in their famous 'double' winning team of 1961?

7 MUSIC: For whom did Gustav Holst write *St Paul's Suite* in 1912?

8 SCIENCE: What is measured by a sphygmomanometer?

9 THE ARTS: Which poet had the Christian names Thomas Stearns?

10 FILM, TV & RADIO: Which TV character does Robert Guillaume play?

11 NATURAL HISTORY: Which animal charges backwards when attacked?

12 MISCELLANY: What is a hypotenuse?

▶ QUIZMASTER: What is a Denver Boot?

ANSWERS 161

1 Chemotherapy.

2 Circumnavigate.

3 The first motorcycle.

4 They were the first animals to fly in a balloon.

5 Constantine The Great.

6 Zaheer Abbas.

7 Ebony and Ivory (1982, with Paul McCartney).

8 Because light travels faster than sound.

9 The Marshalsea.

10 Mae West.

11 Six.

12 Cosmonauts.

■ The apple.

ANSWERS 162

1 12.

2 Pennsylvania.

3 News.

4 The canal system.

5 The Suez crisis.

6 Bill Brown.

7 For the orchestra of St Paul's Girls' School, Hammersmith, at which he was music master.

8 Blood pressure.

9 T.S. Eliot.

10 Benson.

11 The porcupine.

12 The longest side of a right-angled triangle.

■ A parking clamp.

TRIVIA QUIZ 163

1 MISCELLANY: Which river is reputed to be haunted by the Lorelei?

2 GEOGRAPHY & TRAVEL: Where is the Alhambra?

3 PEOPLE: Who presides over debates in the House Of Commons?

4 INVENTIONS: What did Sir Humphrey Davy invent in 1815?

5 HISTORY: What have Roman siege armies and the Royal Navy used in aggression?

6 SPORT: Which jockey's first Derby winner was Never Say Die?

7 MUSIC: Who had a childhood fantasy that she was really Marilyn Monroe's daughter?

8 SCIENCE: What do pterylologists study?

9 THE ARTS: For whom were the tramps Estragon and Vladimir waiting?

10 FILM, TV & RADIO: Who said 'Gentlemen, kindly include me out'?

11 NATURAL HISTORY: What are ornithophilous flowers?

12 MISCELLANY: A TV series based on a modern classic featured Yorkshire's Castle Howard in the title role. What was it called?

▶ QUIZMASTER: The Benedictine monks of Mont St Michel, Brittany once owned a remarkably similar hill-island in Cornwall. What is it called?

TRIVIA QUIZ 164

1 MISCELLANY: What is the name of the art movement which uses small dots and brush strokes to create a large picture?

2 GEOGRAPHY & TRAVEL: What 'odius column' was opened to the public in 1898?

3 PEOPLE: Why did islanders from Tristan da Cunha arrive in Britain in 1961?

4 INVENTIONS: What did Elisha Otis invent in 1853?

5 HISTORY: Which MP introduced a bill in 1876 making a loading line on ships compulsory?

6 SPORT: Who was England's goalkeeper in the 1966 World Cup winning side?

7 MUSIC: Which instrument was invented in 1846?

8 SCIENCE: After oxygen, what is the second most plentiful element on our planet?

9 THE ARTS: Which flesh-eating monster was slain by Beowulf?

10 FILM, TV & RADIO: How old was Peggy Ashcroft when she won her first Oscar?

11 NATURAL HISTORY: What animal found in Britain is sometimes called the foul-mart?

12 MISCELLANY: What is the poorest nation of South America?

▶ QUIZMASTER: What language is spoken in Bulgaria?

ANSWERS 163

1 The Rhine.

2 At Grenada in Spain.

3 The Speaker.

4 The Miners' safety lamp.

5 The catapult.

6 Lester Piggott's.

7 Blondie's Debbie Harry.

8 Feathers.

9 Godot.

10 Samuel Goldwyn.

11 Flowers pollinated by birds.

12 *Brideshead Revisited*.

■ St Michael's Mount.

ANSWERS 164

1 Pointillism.

2 The Eiffel Tower.

3 The island was evacuated because of volcanic eruption.

4 The passenger lift.

5 Samuel Plimsoll.

6 Gordon Banks.

7 The saxophone.

8 Silicon.

9 Grendel.

10 77.

11 The polecat (because of the odour it gives out when frightened).

12 Bolivia.

■ Bulgarian.

TRIVIA QUIZ 165

1 MISCELLANY: Who won £85,010 in libel damages and costs against *Private Eye* in 1983?

2 GEOGRAPHY & TRAVEL: Where are the Elgin Marbles?

3 PEOPLE: Who was the founder of the South African Students' Association who died while under arrest in 1977?

4 INVENTIONS: What process did Nicholas Appart develop after discovering that you could preserve fruit by sealing it in a jar and boiling it?

5 HISTORY: In which country were the Mau-Mau active?

6 SPORT: Which sport makes use of a balance beam?

7 MUSIC: Who released a 14 minute video for a six minute pop song?

8 SCIENCE: For every 500 red blood corpuscles, how many white ones do we have?

9 THE ARTS: How was Charles Lutwidge Dodson better known?

10 FILM, TV & RADIO: Who explained the secrets of *Life On Earth*?

11 NATURAL HISTORY: Which bird lays its eggs in other birds' nests?

12 MISCELLANY: What colour is amethyst?

▶ QUIZMASTER: On the banks of which mighty river did a Spanish explorer spot a group of native female warriors in the 1540s?

TRIVIA QUIZ 166

1 MISCELLANY: Which Greek god was Zeus' Number Two?

2 GEOGRAPHY & TRAVEL: To which holiday tour operator do the subsidiaries Sovereign and Enterprise belong?

3 PEOPLE: What did Kiri te Kanawa do at the wedding of the Prince and Princess of Wales?

4 INVENTIONS: What colour does blue, red and green light make?

5 HISTORY: In which Turkish town was St Paul born?

6 SPORT: Which goalkeeper broke his neck in the 1956 Cup Final?

7 MUSIC: What song by The Mighty Diamonds was a hit for the British group Musical Youth?

8 SCIENCE: The water of which sea has four ounces of salt for every pint?

9 THE ARTS: Which legendary beauty does Mephistopheles procure for Dr Faustus?

10 FILM, TV & RADIO: Who played Captain Scott in *The Last Place On Earth*?

11 NATURAL HISTORY: In which sea do sea eels lay their eggs?

12 MISCELLANY: What is the main ingredient of the puffin's diet?

▶ QUIZMASTER: To what did the ancient papyrus-exporting town of Byblos, near present-day Beirut give its name?

ANSWERS 165

1 Sir James Goldsmith.

2 The British Museum.

3 Steve Biko.

4 The canning process.

5 Kenya.

6 Gymnastics.

7 Michael Jackson (*Thriller*).

8 One.

9 Lewis Carroll.

10 David Attenborough.

11 The cuckoo.

12 Purple.

■ The Amazon (hence its name).

ANSWERS 166

1 Apollo.

2 British Airways.

3 Sing.

4 White.

5 Tarsus.

6 Bert Trautmann.

7 'Pass The Dutchie'.

8 The Dead Sea.

9 Helen Of Troy.

10 Martin Shaw.

11 In the Sargasso Sea.

12 Fish.

■ *The Bible*.

TRIVIA QUIZ 167

1 **MISCELLANY:** What was the 57 mile long Marcia, built by the Romans?

2 **GEOGRAPHY & TRAVEL:** Which is the second biggest Maltese island?

3 **PEOPLE:** Who did a series of World War II radio talks called *Postscripts*?

4 **INVENTIONS:** Who was handed the first complete printed copy of his book *On The Revolutions Of The Celestial Spheres* on the last day of his life?

5 **HISTORY:** Who made the Great Trek across South Africa?

6 **SPORT:** Which nationality is the football club Anderlecht?

7 **MUSIC:** Who sung the theme tune of *Ghostbusters*?

8 **SCIENCE:** How much would a one metre cube of platinum weigh (to the nearest ton)?

9 **THE ARTS:** Who broke off his engagement to Natasha Rostov in *War and Peace?*

10 **FILM, TV & RADIO:** Which war film used the music of The Doors and Wagner?

11 **NATURAL HISTORY:** What is the generic term for the following: king, emperor, jackass?

12 **MISCELLANY:** Who built a city in India called Bucephala in memory of his horse?

▶ **QUIZMASTER:** What is the permanent population of the continent of Antarctica?

TRIVIA QUIZ 168

1 What do the rose and the apple have in common?

2 **GEOGRAPHY & TRAVEL:** Why do the Swiss have no navy?

3 **PEOPLE:** Which American president said: 'I let down my friends, I let down my country, I let down our system of government'?

4 **INVENTIONS:** What two metals are combined to make brass?

5 **HISTORY:** Which leader introduced reforms in Czechoslovakia in the late 60s?

6 **SPORT:** What physical activity comes naturally to most animals but has to be taught to humans?

7 **MUSIC:** Who sang 'Kissing To Be Clever'?

8 **SCIENCE:** Is phlogiston, first defined by 17th century chemists, a real substance or not?

9 **THE ARTS:** Who left *The Weir Of Hermiston* unfinished?

10 **FILM, TV & RADIO:** Who said 'There is no terror in a bang, only in the anticipation of it'?

11 **NATURAL HISTORY:** What is a snake doing when it sloughs?

12 **MISCELLANY:** What material did the Ancient Greeks call 'elektron', from which we get the word electricity'?

▶ **QUIZMASTER:** Which country is 2,790 miles long but only 250 miles wide at its widest point?

ANSWERS 167

1 An aquaduct.

2 Gozo.

3 JB Priestley.

4 Copernicus.

5 The Boers.

6 Belgian.

7 Ray Parker Junior.

8 20 tons.

9 Prince Andrei Bolkonsky.

10 *Apocalypse Now*.

11 Penguin.

12 Alexander The Great.

■ Zero.

ANSWERS 168

1 They belong to the same family.

2 They have no coast.

3 Richard Nixon.

4 Zinc and copper.

5 Alexander Dubček.

6 Swimming.

7 Boy George (of Culture Club).

8 It's not. Materials which burnt were supposed to contain it.

9 Robert Louis Stevenson.

10 Alfred Hitchcock.

11 Casting its skin.

12 Amber.

■ Chile.

TRIVIA QUIZ 169

1 MISCELLANY: From which London palace did the BBC transmit the first TV service?

2 GEOGRAPHY & TRAVEL: Which city is served by Schipol Airport?

3 PEOPLE: Which British author had the Christian names John Ronald Reuel?

4 INVENTIONS: What is the problem caused by the excessive streamlining of fast cars, which the aerofoil counteracts?

5 HISTORY: How many kings named George have ruled Britain?

6 SPORT: Which jockey became a best-selling thriller writer?

7 MUSIC: Name one of Frank Sinatra's two solo British number one hits.

8 SCIENCE: What is the brightest common object in the sky, after the sun and the moon?

9 THE ARTS: Which philosopher is buried in Highgate Cemetery, London?

10 FILM, TV & RADIO: In which TV series did Nick Nolte play Tom Jordache?

11 NATURAL HISTORY: Where do newts spend their adult life?

12 MISCELLANY: What is the blue in blue cheese?

▶ **QUIZMASTER:** Five squared equals 25. What other number when squared gives the answer 25?

TRIVIA QUIZ 170

1 MISCELLANY: What would you keep in a bandolier?

2 GEOGRAPHY & TRAVEL: By what name is the country of Bechuanaland now known?

3 PEOPLE: Which nation has the highest newspaper readership per head of population?

4 INVENTIONS: Who discovered the binomial theory at the age of 21?

5 HISTORY: What did Sir John Harington design for his own home in 1589?

6 SPORT: What game was regularly played at the Artillery Ground, London in the 18th century?

7 MUSIC: What was David Bowie's first hit?

8 SCIENCE: The temperature of the sun has to be achieved to create what potentially useful nuclear reaction?

9 THE ARTS: Which major novel takes place entirely on the day of June 16, 1904?

10 FILM, TV & RADIO: Who played Jim Rockford in *The Rockford Files*?

11 NATURAL HISTORY: Which animal always gives birth to identical quadruplets?

12 MISCELLANY: From what kind of yarn is the best velvet made?

▶ **QUIZMASTER:** Which country encloses Berlin completely?

ANSWERS 169

1 Alexandra Palace.

2 Amsterdam.

3 JRR Tolkien.

4 Lift (or the car beginning to take off).

5 Six.

6 Dick Francis.

7 'Strangers In The Night' and 'Three Coins In The Fountain'.

8 Venus.

9 Karl Marx.

10 *Rich Man, Poor Man*.

11 On land.

12 Mould.

■ Minus five.

ANSWERS 170

1 Ammunition.

2 Botswana.

3 Britain.

4 Isaac Newton.

5 The first water closet.

6 Cricket.

7 'Space Oddity'.

8 Nuclear fusion.

9 James Joyce's *Ulysses*.

10 James Garner.

11 The armadillo.

12 Silk.

■ East Germany.

TRIVIA QUIZ 171

1 MISCELLANY: On which finger is the wedding ring worn in Germany and France?

2 GEOGRAPHY & TRAVEL: To which country do the Canary Isles belong?

3 PEOPLE: Which European country has the largest population?

4 INVENTIONS: What machine did the German engineer Karl Benz first produce in 1885?

5 HISTORY: Who led the first major movement of fascists in Europe?

6 SPORT: What sport was created when William Webb Ellis violated the rules of football in 1823?

7 MUSIC: Who was Martha, in the McCartney hit 'Martha My Dear'?

8 SCIENCE: What did Galileo demonstrate when he dropped objects from the top of the Leaning Tower Of Pisa?

9 THE ARTS: Which quartet ends with *The Division Of The Spoils?*

10 FILM, TV & RADIO: What was the name of Charlie Chaplin's film satire of Nazi Germany?

11 NATURAL HISTORY: Why do you never hear gardeners complaining about moles in Ireland?

12 MISCELLANY: What would happen to you if you were tonsured?

▶ **QUIZMASTER:** Whose epitaph reads 'If you seek his memorial, look around you'?

TRIVIA QUIZ 172

1 MISCELLANY: What happened to the Mona Lisa in 1911?

2 GEOGRAPHY & TRAVEL: Which country ruled Papua New Guinea, until its independence in 1975?

3 PEOPLE: What physical characteristic did Toulouse-Lautrec, Debbie Reynolds and St Francis Of Assisi have in common?

4 INVENTIONS: By what name was the 'ordinary bicycle' of 1871 more popularly known?

5 HISTORY: What did Aztec Indians smoke in 1522?

6 SPORT: Which goalkeeper was the first to win the European Footballer Of The Year award?

7 MUSIC: What do Hari Georgeson, George O'Hara Smith and Son of Harry share?

8 SCIENCE: What is an alloy?

9 THE ARTS: What is the name of the dog in *Peter Pan?*

10 FILM, TV & RADIO: Which actress got her big break when she was noticed in an ice cream parlour by the editor of the Hollywood Reporter in 1936?

11 NATURAL HISTORY: How do amphibians, like frogs and toads breathe?

12 MISCELLANY: How old would Marilyn Monroe be in 1986 if she had lived?

▶ **QUIZMASTER:** Where would you find the following typical patterns: arch, tented arch, radial loop, ulnar loop, whorl?

ANSWERS 171

1 On the third finger of the right hand.

2 Spain.

3 West Germany.

4 A petrol-powered motor car.

5 Benito Mussolini.

6 Rugby football.

7 His old English sheep dog.

8 That objects of different weights fall at the same rate.

9 The Raj Quartet.

10 *The Great Dictator*.

11 Because there aren't any moles in Ireland.

12 The crown of your head would be shaven (like a monk's).

■ Christopher Wren's (inscribed over the north door of St Paul's Cathedral).

ANSWERS 172

1 It was stolen.

2 Australia.

3 Their height (they were all 5' 1" tall).

4 The penny farthing.

5 Tobacco.

6 Lev Yashin of the USSR.

7 They are all recording pseudonyms used by George Harrison.

8 A mixture of two or more metals.

9 Nana.

10 Lana Turner.

11 Through the skin.

12 60.

■ Fingerprints.

TRIVIA QUIZ 173

1 MISCELLANY: Which unfortunate Greek god gave his name to the word 'tantalize'?

2 GEOGRAPHY & TRAVEL: Which region is milder, the Arctic or the Antarctic?

3 PEOPLE: Who said: 'If thought corrupts language, language can also corrupt thought'?

4 INVENTIONS: Who invented the electric battery?

5 HISTORY: Arthur Wellesley is more often referred to by one of his titles – which one?

6 SPORT: Which father and son have both played cricket for England?

7 MUSIC: Who wrote 'Keep the Home Fires Burning'?

8 SCIENCE: In which learned discipline would you expect to come across the Sieve of Eratosthenes?

9 THE ARTS: Which Victorian was Poet Laureate for 40 years?

10 FILM, TV & RADIO: Which TV series invented The Flying Fickle Finger of Fate Award?

11 NATURAL HISTORY: The branch of which tree is a symbol of peace?

12 MISCELLANY: Which British city is hoping to host the 1992 Olympic Games?

▶ **QUIZMASTER:** What famous structure connects a state prison with a Doge's palace?

TRIVIA QUIZ 174

1 MISCELLANY: In which city was the world's first underground railway?

2 GEOGRAPHY & TRAVEL: What is the official language of Brazil?

3 PEOPLE: Who enjoyed a first flight in Concorde on 6 August 1985?

4 INVENTIONS: By what other name do we usually refer to radio detection and ranging?

5 HISTORY: What was King Ethelred II's nickname?

6 SPORT: Where is the 2,000 Guineas run?

7 MUSIC: The rediscovery of whose piano rags made ragtime music popular again in the second half of this century?

8 SCIENCE: In experiments, what is a pipette used for?

9 THE ARTS: Which children's story takes place in St Petersburg, Missouri?

10 FILM, TV & RADIO: In the TV cartoon series *Tom & Jerry* which one is the cat and which the mouse?

11 NATURAL HISTORY: What is the difference between almonds of white flowering trees and those of pink flowering trees?

12 MISCELLANY: On what object would you find a barb, a shaft and a quill?

▶ **QUIZMASTER:** What did the school careers of Sarah Bernhardt, Humphrey Bogart, Leon Trotsky, Benito Mussolini and Salvador Dali have in common?

ANSWERS 173

1 Tantalus, whose fate was to be surrounded by food and water but unable to reach either.

2 The Arctic.

3 George Orwell.

4 Alessandro Volta.

5 Duke of Wellington.

6 Colin Cowdrey and Chris Cowdrey.

7 Ivor Novello.

8 Mathematics (it is a method of finding prime numbers).

9 Alfred, Lord Tennyson.

10 *Rowan & Martin's Laugh-In.*

11 The olive.

12 Birmingham.

■ The Bridge of Sighs, Venice.

ANSWERS 174

1 London.

2 Portuguese.

3 The Queen Mother.

4 Radar.

5 The Unready.

6 Newmarket.

7 Scott Joplin.

8 A pipette is a slender glass tube used for transferring or measuring out known volumes of liquid.

9 *Tom Sawyer.*

10 Tom is the cat and Jerry is the mouse.

11 Almonds from white flowering trees are bitter.

12 A feather.

■ They were all expelled or suspended.

TRIVIA QUIZ 175

1 MISCELLANY: Its French name 'dindon' means from India, but where did the turkey really originate?

2 GEOGRAPHY & TRAVEL: What is the lowest land surface on earth?

3 PEOPLE: Which member of the government resigned after a scandal in 1983?

4 INVENTIONS: Which Greek scientist invented a water-raising screw and is remembered for his work on buoyancy.

5 HISTORY: In which year was the revolution in Iran?

6 SPORT: Who did Boris Becker defeat in the men's singles finals at Wimbledon in 1985?

7 MUSIC: Which composer is especially associated with good food?

8 SCIENCE: What is being defined: 'An orbiting device which transmits scientific information or is used for communication'?

9 THE ARTS: What is the name of the 1982 Booker Prize winner which caused a controversy about whether or not it was a novel?

10 FILM, TV & RADIO: Which film won the Academy Award for best film in 1984?

11 NATURAL HISTORY: What is the only armoured mammal?

12 MISCELLANY: What kind of vehicle did Walt Disney, Ernest Hemingway, Dashiell Hammett and W. Somerset Maugham all drive in the First World War?

▶ QUIZMASTER: How many towns in Great Britain are called Newport?

TRIVIA QUIZ 176

1 MISCELLANY: What percentage (to the nearest 5) of Egypt's total area is settled and/or cultivated?

2 GEOGRAPHY & TRAVEL: What is Europe's longest river?

3 PEOPLE: What was Aristotle Onassis' learned middle name?

4 INVENTIONS: Which well-known modern writer is descended from the creator of the dahlia?

5 HISTORY: Name one of the two democratic republics which existed by 1800.

6 SPORT: Which is the only non-league football team ever to win the F.A. Cup?

7 MUSIC: Who performed the last act in the British Live Aid concert before the grand finale?

8 SCIENCE: In light or pigment, what colour is cyan?

9 THE ARTS: Who wrote *Notre Dame de Paris*?

10 FILM, TV & RADIO: What is the last line of *Some Like it Hot*?

11 NATURAL HISTORY: Where in Britain can you see a grape vine that is certified 300 years old?

12 MISCELLANY: King Arthur's sword was called Excalibur. What was the more plebian-sounding name of his spear?

▶ QUIZMASTER: What number when increased by 10%, the result of which is decreased by 10%, gives you 99?

189

ANSWERS 175

1 North and Central America.

2 The Dead Sea shoreline (1289 feet below sea level).

3 Cecil Parkinson.

4 Archimedes.

5 1979.

6 Kevin Curran.

7 Rossini.

8 A satellite.

9 *Schindler's Ark*.

10 *Amadeus*.

11 The armadillo.

12 An ambulance.

■ Eleven.

ANSWERS 176

1 3 per cent.

2 The Volga (2290 miles long).

3 Socrates.

4 Roald Dahl. Dahlias were named after one of his ancestors.

5 France and the U.S.A.

6 Tottenham Hotspur in 1901.

7 Paul McCartney.

8 Blue.

9 Victor Hugo.

10 Nobody's perfect!

11 Hampton Court.

12 Ron.

■ 100.

TRIVIA QUIZ 177

1 MISCELLANY: What links Nellie Melba, the singer, Anna Pavlova, the dancer and Queen Charlotte, wife of George III?

2 GEOGRAPHY & TRAVEL: Which motorway links Glasgow and Edinburgh?

3 PEOPLE: What nationality was Madame Curie?

4 INVENTIONS: What does the Bessemer process do?

5 HISTORY: Whose case did Charles VII reopen in 1455, 24 years after she had been sentenced to death?

6 SPORT: In which sport do you find hazard chases, a grille and a winning gallery?

7 MUSIC: What is the real name of Boy George?

8 SCIENCE: In which branch of mathematics do you get a result of zero when you add the sides of a triangle?

9 THE ARTS: Which biblical epic was written by a former governor of New Mexico?

10 FILM, TV & RADIO: Which star of British films was born in the Old Kent Road and had the unromantic-sounding real name of Maurice Micklewhite?

11 NATURAL HISTORY: What sort of acid is in an ant's sting?

12 MISCELLANY: Which drink, beloved of 19th century Parisians, was flavoured with wormwood and is now illegal owing to its devastating effects?

▶ QUIZMASTER: Glasgow gained a major new museum in the 1980s. What is it called?

TRIVIA QUIZ 178

1 MISCELLANY: How did Sir Henry Tate, founder of the Tate Gallery, make his fortune?

2 GEOGRAPHY & TRAVEL: What is the capital of Algeria?

3 PEOPLE: Which tribe did chief Cetewayo lead to a victory over the British in 1879?

4 INVENTIONS: What card game is said to have been invented by the poet Sir John Suckling?

5 HISTORY: What is the 25,000 year old treasure of Altamira?

6 SPORT: With which sport do you associate the following positions: gully, long on and third man?

7 MUSIC: What was Anna Pavlova's most famous balletic role?

8 SCIENCE: How many fluid ounces are there in an English pint?

9 THE ARTS: Which out-dated novel begins 'It was a bright cold in April and the clocks were striking thirteen'?

10 FILM, TV & RADIO: Which classic film finally had a sequel made to it 46 years after its release?

11 NATURAL HISTORY: What was the biggest dinosaur, in terms of overall length?

12 MISCELLANY: In which city is Knotty Ash?

▶ QUIZMASTER: Estimate, to the nearest 100 works, the total output of Picasso's career.

1 They have all had puddings named after them.

2 The M8.

3 Polish.

4 It is the process by which steel is made.

5 Joan of Arc's.

6 Real tennis.

7 George O'Dowd.

8 Vectors.

9 *Ben Hur* (by General Lew Wallace).

10 Michael Caine.

11 Formic acid.

12 Absinthe.

■ The Burrell Collection.

ANSWERS 178

1 In sugar, alongside Mr Lyle.

2 Algiers.

3 The Zulus.

4 Cribbage.

5 A cave painting of a bison head.

6 Cricket.

7 *The Dying Swan.*

8 20.

9 *Nineteen Eighty-Four.*

10 *The Wizard of Oz;* the sequel was called *Return to Oz.*

11 Diplodocus, at more than 87 feet long.

12 Liverpool.

■ 147,800.